OCEAN ANIMALS AND THEIR ECOSYSTEMS

OCEAN ANIMALS

AND THEIR ECOSYSTEMS

A Nature Reference Book for Kids

Dr. Erica Colón

ROCKRIDGE
PRESS

Interior and Cover Designer: Erin Yeung
Art Producer: Janice Ackerman
Editor: Cathy Hennessy
Production Editor: Mia Moran

Custom illustration by Sara Lynn Cramb: p. 16-19, p. 23 top, p. 43 bottom, p. 146, 148, 149 bottom

Cover photography courtesy of iStock, clockwise: tane-mahuta; cmeder; Andrea Izzotti; Olga Rakhm

Backcover photography: clockwise: Andrew Woodward/Alamy Stock Photo; mauritius images GmbH/Alamy Stock Photo; lelmvilla/iStock; Isabelle Kuehn/Shutterstock

Author photo: © 2020 Hannah Aleece Photography

ISBN: Print 978-1-64611-640-9 | eBook 978-1-64611-641-6

R0

To my explorers, Ava, Dani, and Lincoln—
I cannot wait to share the beautiful places and
animals this world has to show you.

Contents

Introduction

Water from the world's oceans covers 71 percent of Earth's surface—that's why it is called "the blue planet." The ocean is full of wild and beautiful creatures that call it their home. This book is all about them.

The oceans form an interconnected system, making a huge realm that currently holds around 232,000 marine species. That's a lot, but marine biologists say that more than 90 percent of the ocean's species are still undiscovered. There could still be over two million species out there. How is this possible? First, you need to understand when we started *really* looking.

History reveals that people living near the ocean discovered that it held many resources, such as food for eating and shells for tools. Many of the creatures they found lived close to shore and along coastlines, like those you'll learn about in chapter 3. People who ventured farther on long ocean voyages usually set out to explore distant lands and map out the oceans, not to study below the waves. But these early voyagers were helpful. They gave future explorers reliable maps that included lines of **longitude** and **latitude** to **navigate** the seas better.

It wasn't until around the 1800s that scientists came along on voyages. The scientists were there to study any new marine **organisms** they found. Since then, with the help of navigational instruments, technology, and ocean-ready equipment, amazing discoveries have been made. We've explored a lot, but more than 80 percent of the ocean is still yet to be seen by humans. That's a lot of space on this planet that remains a mystery.

Although we have barely scratched the surface, marine scientists keep pushing to learn more. At every layer of the ocean, there are living things. Each **ecosystem** or habitat will determine what organisms can be found. Every ecosystem has distinctive characteristics—such as light, temperature, **salinity**, tides, currents, and **pressure**—that allow an organism to live there or not. Pressure, for example, is the force exerted by the water surrounding something in the ocean. Pressure changes dramatically with depth. Marine species that live in the deep, such as those you'll read about in chapter 6, have adapted to the pressure and can survive. Surface dwellers would not be able to live at the same depth.

It's extraordinary that there are so many creatures waiting to be discovered. At the same time, research suggests that the number of species in the ocean is decreasing. Many marine ecosystems are suffering from pollution, rising sea temperatures, and a decline in health. It doesn't have to be this way. I know you are reading this book because, just like me and my family, you are fascinated by the ocean and care for the animals in it. When I was a high school science teacher, my marine biology students and I were offered an opportunity to volunteer on an ocean research vessel off the coast of Oahu, Hawaii. This amazing experience was eye-opening. Information collected by scientists gives people a much better understanding of this world. It also showed us some of the challenges that have occurred due to pollution and coastal development. As humans, we can make better choices to help protect and preserve ocean ecosystems. Throughout this book, I'll be sharing my favorite marine creatures, along with conservation ideas that you can do today to start making a positive impact on the ocean. What an honor it is to have an ocean protector like you in this world!

NOTE ON FACT BOX DATA

The International Union for Conservation of Nature's (IUCN) Red List of Threatened Species is the world's most complete information source on the global conservation status of animal, fungus, and plant species. The animal conservation status given in the fact boxes throughout the book uses the following IUCN Red List threat categories:

Critically Endangered: Facing an extremely high risk of **extinction** in the wild.

Endangered: Facing a very high risk of extinction in the wild.

Vulnerable: Facing a high risk of extinction in the wild.

Near Threatened: Likely to qualify for a threatened category in the near future.

Least Concern: Low-risk category.

Data Deficient: Not enough data to make an assessment.

Not Evaluated: Has not yet been assessed.

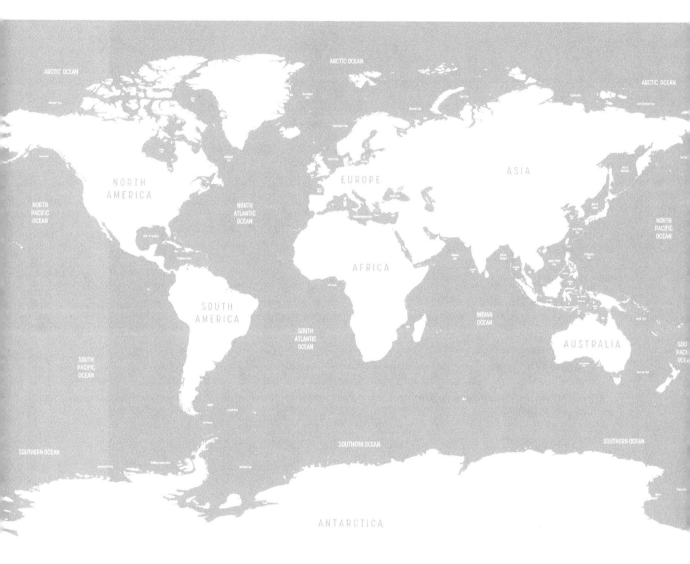

Oceans of the World

How many oceans are there? On Earth, there is one global ocean, but it's divided into different regions. Traditionally, the oceans of the world were treated like four separate bodies of water. From largest to smallest, they are the Pacific Ocean, Atlantic Ocean, Indian Ocean, and Arctic Ocean. However, the world's oceans are actually interconnected. You can see this if you hold a globe and look at the world from the South Pole. From this perspective, the Pacific, Atlantic, and Indian Oceans are large basins that branch off a continuous body of water that surrounds Antarctica. This fifth ocean basin is called the Southern Ocean. It is now recognized as an ocean by most countries, including the United States.

TOTAL AREA AND AVERAGE DEPTH OF THE OCEAN BASINS

OCEAN	AREA MILLIONS OF SQUARE MILES (SQUARE KILOMETERS)	AVERAGE DEPTH FEET (METERS)	DEEPEST PLACE FEET (METERS)	PROPORTION OF GLOBAL OCEAN (%)
PACIFIC	60 (155)	13,700 (4,100)	Challenger Deep in Mariana Trench 35,840 (10,924)	47
ATLANTIC	29 (75)	12,881 (3,926)	Milwaukee Deep in Puerto Rico Trench 28,231 (8605)	23
INDIAN	26 (68)	13,800 (4,210)	Java Trench 23,812 (7,258)	20
ARCTIC	5.4 (14)	4,900 (1,500)	Malloy Deep 17,880 (5,450)	4
SOUTHERN	7 (20)	14,760 (4,500)	South Sandwich Trench 23,737 (7,235)	6

Pacific Ocean

The Pacific is hands down the largest and deepest of the ocean basins. It contains more than half of the liquid water on Earth and covers about 60 million square miles—all of the Earth's continents could fit inside it! The floor of the Pacific is remarkable—its **tectonic plates** are in constant motion, forming deep trenches in some areas and mountain chains in others. **Seamounts**, or underwater volcanoes, are scattered throughout the Pacific and have hardly been studied. The few that have been are home to hundreds of species, with about a third of them being new to science.

How Did the Pacific Get Its Name?

In November 1520, Ferdinand Magellan and his crew entered an unfamiliar body of water that he called *pacific*, which means peaceful. He felt this ocean had a calmness compared to the treacherous waters he'd just crossed in the Atlantic. His crew celebrated, thinking they were close to their destination. Little did they know they were entering the largest ocean in the world.

Ring of Fire

Along the plate boundaries of the Pacific lies approximately 24,900 miles (40,000 kilometers) of active volcanoes and frequent earthquakes. This appropriately named Ring of Fire is where 75 percent of Earth's volcanoes are located and where 90 percent of the world's earthquakes occur. These frequent dramatic events are due to the movement of the tectonic plates along the boundaries.

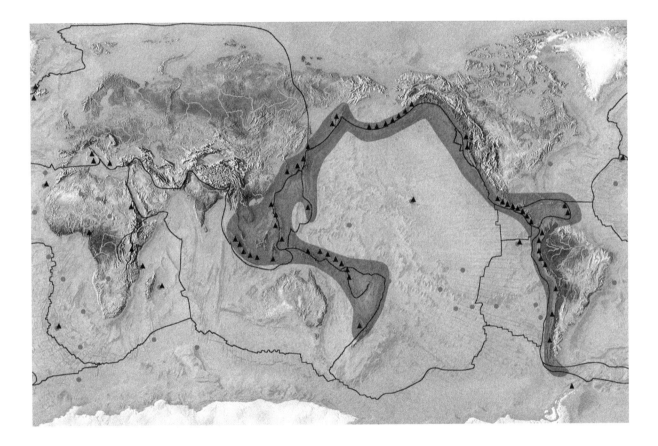

Atlantic Ocean

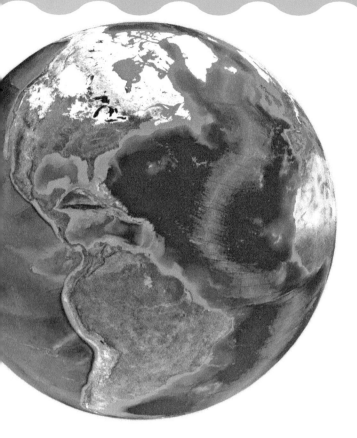

The warm and cold currents circulating between the North and South Atlantic act like a giant conveyor belt influencing weather around the world. Scientists estimate that it takes water 500 years to make one turn around this conveyor belt. The Atlantic is also infamous for some of the world's most massive hurricanes. These are fueled by the warm currents mixing with wind from the **jet streams** sweeping across the surface.

Mid-Atlantic Ridge

Along the Atlantic floor lies a huge mountain range that extends the entire length of the ocean. This is a portion of an oceanic ridge that circles the whole planet. In some places, the top of the ridge reaches above sea level. There it forms islands, such as Iceland.

Silfra Fissure

The Silfra Fissure is the only place in the world where a person can dive between two tectonic plates—North American and Eurasian—and touch two continents at the same time! This **fissure** formed between the two plates in 1789 because of an earthquake. The two plates continue to drift apart about two centimeters per year.

Indian Ocean

The Indian Ocean, unlike the Atlantic and Pacific, does not extend to Arctic waters. Due to its location within the tropics, most of the Indian Ocean has warm **surface temperatures**. Along its coasts are several well-defined ecosystems including coral reefs, **estuaries**, salt marshes, and the largest mangrove forests in the world.

Monsoon

The northern Indian Ocean has a seasonal wind called a **monsoon**. This wind is unique in that it blows from the dry northeast during winter months, then reverses and brings rain from the wet southwest during the summer months.

Tsunami

The Java Trench in the Indian Ocean is the world's second-longest trench after the Mariana Trench. It stretches 2,800 miles (4,500 kilometers). In 2004, an undersea earthquake began in this trench, causing a series of devastating giant waves called **tsunamis**, which hit coastal towns.

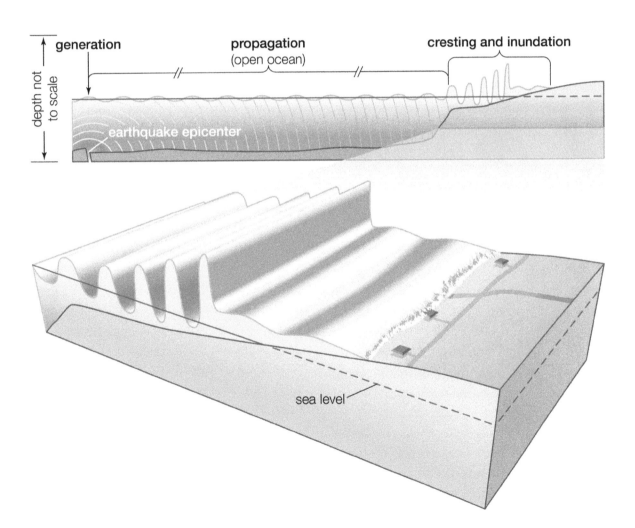

Arctic Ocean

The smallest and shallowest of the basins, the Arctic Ocean, is almost surrounded by continents and islands. Even though it's located in a polar region, the Arctic has no permanent sea ice. Winter ice melts during the summer. When the ice melts, it releases trapped, often frozen organisms and dead plankton. These dead creatures feed a variety of soft corals, clams, and **isopods**, which are then eaten by crabs, walruses, and gray whales.

The Northwest Passage

The Northwest Passage was historically an elusive quest for a shipping route, sometimes trapping ships in ice for months. In the summer of 2007, global warming caused the route to be completely ice-free for the first time in recorded history. Not only could ships voyage from the Atlantic to the Pacific, but species even migrated across the Arctic. Gray whales, which normally only live in the Pacific, found their way to the Mediterranean Sea.

Polar Night

Polar night—when nighttime lasts for more than 24 hours—occurs in the polar regions during the winter months. In the Arctic, it begins around the fall equinox, when the region tilts away from the sun. The darkness lasts for six months, until the spring equinox when the sun starts to show again over the horizon.

Southern Ocean

The Southern Ocean is an extension of all major oceans and circles the entire continent of Antarctica. The **continental shelf** below the surface is surprisingly rich with life, with many species found nowhere else in the world. This unique **biodiversity** is thanks to currents acting as a barrier from the continental shelves of other continents.

The Roaring Forties

The Roaring Forties are westerly winds named for the latitude at which they occur. With no landmass to slow them down, these winds pound the Southern Ocean. Hundreds of years ago, sailors discovered that they could harness these winds to travel faster.

Drake Passage

The Drake Passage is a deep, 600-mile-wide waterway that connects the Atlantic and Pacific Oceans. Waters here are rich in krill, which are shrimp-like **crustaceans** that are the main food source for blue whales, squid, emperor penguins, and crabeater seals. However, it was always a gamble—this latitude also has extreme weather and waves that regularly reach heights of 33 feet (10 meters).

CHAPTER 1
The Open Ocean

The Open Ocean

When we think of the ocean, most of us picture waves breaking at the beach, kayaking along peaceful bays, or looking up at rugged cliffs weathered by crashing waves. However, these familiar waters near shores and coastlines make up just a portion of the world's oceans. The ocean realm is so enormous that most marine life never comes in contact with the shore, the seafloor, or even the water's surface. Welcome to the open ocean.

What Is an Ecosystem?

An ecosystem is made of all living and nonliving things in an area. For example, a coral reef's ecosystem supports various types of corals, urchins, fish, and other animals. However, it also includes nonliving features like sunlight, tides, currents, and nutrients. Ocean ecosystems vary widely, as you will soon read about. Each ecosystem has marine animals and nonliving features that make it unique.

What Is a Habitat?

Habitats are the natural environment where organisms live. Each habitat has characteristic living and nonliving factors. For marine habitats, this includes temperature, salinity, tides, currents, and depth. In each habitat, living things are always interacting, whether it be prey hiding from predators or species cooperating for survival. This book will explore these habitats along with some of the fascinating interactions among marine life.

What Is a Niche?

Each marine species has a unique place in its habitat called its **niche**. A niche includes an animal's habitat, its food source, the time of day it's most active, and other factors specific to that species. For example, tiger sharks and sandbar sharks both live in the same habitat. But they can both survive because they eat fish from different **food webs**, so there is no competition for food.

The Five Layers of the Ocean

The ocean covers most of the inhabitable space on Earth. Scientists have divided it into five different layers.

Sunlight Zone (Epipelagic Zone)

The sunlight zone extends from the surface down to approximately 650 feet (200 meters). It is known as the sunlight zone because there is plenty of sunlight and heat, although both decrease the deeper you go. Most marine animals, such as whales, dolphins, sharks, tunas, and jellyfish, are found in the sunlight zone.

Twilight Zone (Mesopelagic Zone)

From the bottom of the sunlight zone to the point where sunlight cannot reach is the twilight zone. This zone, stretching down to approximately 3,300 feet (1,000 meters) deep, is home to fishes and **invertebrates** such as the swordfish and wolf eel. At nighttime, many swim up to the sunlight zone to hunt and feed.

Midnight Zone (Bathypelagic Zone)

Traveling deeper, the midnight zone is 15 times the size of the sunlight zone, making it the largest ecosystem on Earth. Organisms in this zone live in complete darkness—sunlight cannot reach its depth of 13,000 feet (4,000 meters). Many animals that live here have specialized glowing organs called **photophores**, like those of fireflies, which are used to attract prey, confuse enemies, or find a mate.

Abyssal Zone (Abyssopelagic Zone)

The abyssal zone has crushing pressure and temperatures near freezing. This zone contains over 75 percent of the ocean floor covered with deep, soft **sediments** of mud and ooze. Here, organisms rely almost entirely on food sinking from above. Therefore, many animals here—such as sea stars, hagfish, and giant isopods—are **scavengers**.

ocean surface 0m

approximately 650 ft (200m)

approximately 3,300 ft (1,000m)

approximately 13,000 ft (4,000m)

ocean floor

THE TRENCHES (HADALPELAGIC ZONE)

This zone is unique in that it only exists in certain places around the world—the deep, wide trenches in the ocean floor. The deepest parts of the ocean make up this zone. In spite of the incredible pressure and near-freezing temperatures, life perseveres here. Invertebrates such as starfish, tubeworms, and the bacteria that live inside them have all adapted to this environment in unique ways.

Food Webs

As a krill feasts on a clump of algae, a herring comes along and eats the krill. Suddenly, a giant tuna swallows the herring whole, only to find itself stunned by the tail of a thresher shark, which then enjoys the tuna for its morning meal. This is an example of a typical food chain, showing how energy moves through an ecosystem. However, feeding relationships are a bit more complicated. Different feeding options lead to interconnecting food chains called food webs. For example, even though the herring eats the krill, the krill may also be breakfast for a blue whale in a different food chain.

Sun -->

Phytoplankton
(producer) -->

Krill
(primary consumer) -->

Jellyfish
(secondary consumer) -->

Sea Turtle
(tertiary consumer) -->

Shark
(quaternary consumer) -->

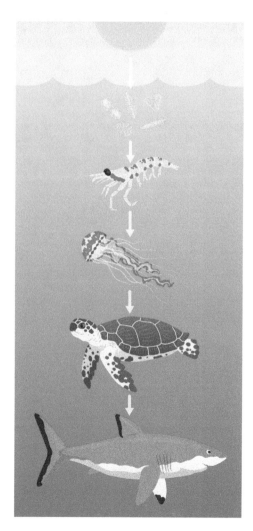

Shark

Humpback Whale

Sea Turtle

Tuna

* Krill

Herring

Octopus

Anchovy

Jellyfish

* Plankton &
Phytoplankton

Shrimp

Squid

* Clams

* Corals & Sponges

*Images Enlarged for detail

Sharks: The Powerful Predators

Sharks are sometimes referred to as "living fossils" because many of them are similar to species that lived more than 100 million years ago. Since that time, their role as a top predator has always helped maintain a healthy ocean. With more than 500 living species, sharks are found throughout the oceans at practically all depths. However, their numbers have declined dramatically due to overfishing and demands for shark fins.

Great White Shark

The largest predatory fish in the world is the great white shark. This aggressive hunter is great at sensing blood three miles away, chasing down some of the fastest prey, and diving to the deep sea. Until recently, they were thought to fear nothing. But researchers have found that they will leave their hunting ground when one animal group enters it: the orcas.

Great White Shark

Size/Weight	16 to 20 ft / 4,000 to 7,000 lbs
Diet	fishes, seals, and other sharks
Speed	35 mph (56 kph)
Status	vulnerable
Life Span	> 70 years

Did You Know?

The largest shark ever roamed the world's oceans roughly 3 million years ago. It was the fearsome megalodon, reaching lengths of 60 feet (18 meters).

Great Hammerhead Shark

The great hammerhead shark hunts alone along the ocean floor for stingrays, octopuses, and other sharks. Its distinct hammer-shaped head helps it find and catch prey. Great hammerheads have been spotted using their heads to pin stingrays to the seafloor, biting them until they stop moving.

Thresher Shark

Thresher sharks, known for having powerful tails longer than the rest of their bodies, hunt by whipping their tails side to side to stun or kill prey. Unfortunately, its tail makes the thresher shark vulnerable to sport fishers, who can effortlessly catch it on their hooks when the shark unknowingly whips it at the bait.

Sharks: Giant Filter Feeders

There are only three species of filter-feeding sharks. Two of them—the whale shark and the basking shark—grow larger than the great white, and the megamouth shark is not far behind. These titans swim along with their giant mouths wide open, feeding on plankton-rich seawater and schools of small fish.

Whale Shark

The graceful whale shark has a white spotted pattern that is unique to each individual. Despite their huge size, they are not dangerous to people. Researchers use software originally designed for star mapping to identify individuals from photographs. Whale sharks are also unique in that they give live birth to hundreds of tiny babies. Other big sharks give birth to a few large young.

Basking Shark

The basking shark feeds in cool oceans, filtering up to 4 million pounds (1,800 metric tons) of water every hour. Its extended gill slits nearly encircle the whole head and make it the most recognizable among sharks.

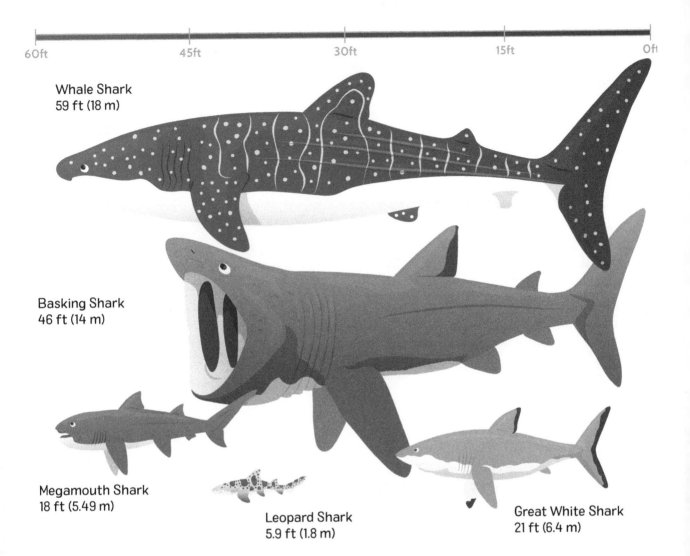

60ft   45ft   30ft   15ft   0ft

Whale Shark
59 ft (18 m)

Basking Shark
46 ft (14 m)

Megamouth Shark
18 ft (5.49 m)

Leopard Shark
5.9 ft (1.8 m)

Great White Shark
21 ft (6.4 m)

Megamouth Shark

Even though it's one of the largest fish in the world, the megamouth shark was only discovered in 1976. Able to grow up to 18 feet in length, this shark earned its name by having a circular mouth 4 feet (1.3 meters) across! These remarkably large mouths are lined with light-producing organs that help attract potential prey.

Baleen Whales

Baleen whales are the largest animals on Earth. They can be found in oceans worldwide, from the polar seas to the tropics. They are named for the long plates of baleen that help them trap and consume their prey. The strong, flexible baleen hangs in a row, like teeth on a comb, from their upper jaws. Their baleen and paired blowholes help distinguish the 15 species of baleen whales—such as the humpback, bowhead, and blue whale—from toothed whales. Though they are enormous, they feed on some of the smallest animals in the ocean—small fish, krill, and plankton.

Humpback Whale

From Antarctica to the Arctic, humpback whales roam the oceans, singing songs that can be heard 20 miles away. Humpback whales travel around 3,000 miles (5,000 kilometers) between their feeding grounds at the poles to birthing and mating grounds in the tropics.

Bowhead Whale

The bowhead whale has a skull that takes up almost a third of its body length—that's enormous considering these whales are, on average, 50 feet (15 meters) long. This giant uses its huge head to break through sea ice in the Arctic waters where it lives.

Blue Whale

It's no secret that the blue whale is the largest animal ever to live in the history of our planet. Reaching lengths of 100 feet (31 meters), this ocean giant can consume 79,000 pounds (36,000 kilograms) a day! Females give birth to calves that are 26 feet (8 meters) in length and drink more than 160 gallons (600 liters) of milk each day for their first year.

Did You Know?

Bowhead whales have the longest baleen plates of all whales, measuring up to 13 feet (4 meters) long!

Blue Whale

Size/Weight	100 ft (31 m) / 190 t
Diet	krill
Speed	31 mph (50 kph) for short bursts, 12 mph (20 kph) for typical travel
Status	endangered
Life Span	80 to 90 years

Toothed Whales

Unlike baleen whales, toothed whales are hunters and capture prey, such as fish, squid, and even seals, with their teeth. Many toothed whales move around in groups called **pods**. Toothed whales—which include sperm whales, orcas, beluga whales, and even dolphins and porpoises—are believed to be some of the most intelligent animals on Earth.

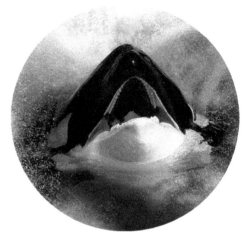

Sperm Whale

The largest of the toothed whales, the sperm whale possesses the most powerful **echo-location** to detect prey in the deep. They can dive to incredible depths and stay down for over an hour. Giant squid is their main food source, but they are known to put up a fight—lots of sperm whales have disk-shaped scars and wounds from squid.

Beluga Whale

The beluga whale is one of only two species in the "white whales" family, the other being its cousin the narwhal. Belugas reside in the Arctic Ocean but have been seen venturing into freshwater rivers. They are called "canaries of the sea" because they make sounds such as squeals, whistles, chirps, and clicks.

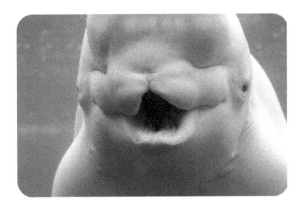

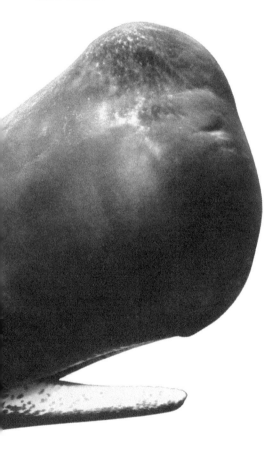

Pilot Whale

Pilot whales form large pods and are named for their behavior of following a "pilot" or a lead whale when traveling long distances. Pilot whales are known for their tendency to strand themselves on beaches. The largest recorded stranding was of about 1,000 whales in 1918. Theories point to the whales having poor echolocation in shallow waters when they follow a food source inshore.

A common sight in the open ocean is well-defined groups of fish called schools. Schools offer protection against predators, making it difficult for a predator to aim for just one fish in a cloud of darting individuals. But this school of jacks is actually the predator—they are more efficient when they attack as a coordinated group.

Dolphins and Porpoises

Most small toothed whales are dolphins or porpoises. The 32 species of dolphin have a distinctive beak with pointed teeth and the appearance of a smile. The six porpoise species have blunt noses and teeth shaped like spades. Dolphins and porpoises are both highly intelligent and generate sound waves to help them navigate and hunt.

Bottlenose Dolphin

Bottlenose dolphins are sleek swimmers that have been known to show off their wave-riding skills among surfers and boaters. These clever mammals sometimes follow fishing boats and take advantage of an easy meal from the leftovers. Bottlenose dolphins work together as a group to round up and surround schools of fish, known as a bait ball, then dive in the middle to feed.

Bottlenose Dolphin

Size/Weight	6.6 to 12.8 ft (2 to 3.9 m) / 330 to 1,400 lbs (150 to 635 kg)
Diet	fishes, squids, and crustaceans
Speed	3 to 22 mph (5 to 35 kph)
Status	least concern
Life Span	40 to 60 years

Spinner Dolphin

The spinner dolphin is the acrobat of the sea. It gets its name for its ability to leap out of the water and spin its body as many as seven times in a row! Biologists believe that while sometimes the dolphins are just being playful, these moves also help them communicate with one another.

Harbor Porpoise

Harbor porpoises are found throughout coastal waters in the Northern Hemisphere. Unfortunately, their preference for shallower waters often gets them caught by accident in commercial fishing nets. Maxing out at lengths of only about 5 feet (1.5 meters), harbor porpoises are among the smallest of the toothed whales.

Jellyfish and Their Relatives

Jellyfish, sea anemones, and their relatives are **cnidarians** that all have **radial symmetry**. This means that if the animal were sliced like a pizza, all pieces would be the same. Cnidarians also do not have heads, fronts, or backs. They do, however, have a centrally located mouth surrounded by tentacles. Specialized cells in the tentacles called **nematocysts** contain a **venomous** barb that can be fired for self-defense or to capture prey.

Moon Jelly

The moon jelly has a round, shallow bell and relatively short tentacles. Found throughout the North Atlantic Ocean, it hunts small invertebrates and occasionally fish. It is also a favorite food of choice for the leatherback turtle and ocean sunfish.

Box Jellyfish

Considered the most venomous marine animal, the box jellyfish—also called sea wasp—has a sting that can cause **paralysis**, heart attacks, or even death. The box jellies have traits that other jellyfish do not—they can swim rather than drift along with a current, and they can see!

Portuguese Man-of-War

The Portuguese man-of-war is commonly mistaken for a jellyfish, but it is not a single animal. It is a **siphonophore**, a colony of four kinds of tiny organisms that depend on one another to live. Each group of organisms is specialized to do a job. For example, one colony forms the gas-filled float while another forms long tentacles to capture prey.

Did You Know?

The lion's mane jellyfish has a bell that can be 8 feet (2.5 meters) across, and tentacles that can stretch over 100 feet (31 meters)— that's the same length as a blue whale!

Seabirds

Seabirds eat marine organisms and only use land for breeding and nesting. They spend a significant part of their lives at sea. They have developed a range of characteristics useful in the marine environment. Salt glands just above the eyes help many seabirds remove salt from the water and secrete it through their nostrils. Specialized feathers and wings help seabirds cover long distances, act as camouflage, and are waterproof to help them float and stay warm. Seabirds are vital to marine ecosystems and help scientists monitor the ocean's health.

Albatross

The albatross enjoys a long life, sometimes over 50 years. It takes 3 to 10 months after being born for an albatross to get all its feathers, but once it does, it spends the next 5 to 10 years gliding over the ocean without ever touching land.

Albatross

Size/Weight	wingspan of 6.5 to 11 ft / up to 22 lbs
Diet	squids, fishes, and crustaceans
Speed	up to 67 mph (107 kph)
Status	endangered to critically endangered
Life Span	> 50 years

Did You Know?

The wandering albatross has the longest wingspan of any bird—up to 11 feet!

Blue-Footed Booby

The blue-footed booby's bright blue feet are its most distinctive feature and play an important role in mating. Females choose males with brighter-colored feet after being shown a high-strutting dance, followed by a presentation of a gift, usually a stick or stone.

Pelican

The pelican likes to feed on small fish like anchovies and silversides. When it spots a school of fish, it feeds by diving down and plunging into the water. Pelicans differ from other diving birds—instead of chasing prey underwater, they take a large gulp of water, hoping for one full of fish.

Great Pacific Garbage Patch

4 Things We Can Do About It

An estimated 2 million tons of plastic enters the ocean each year from rivers. Halfway between Hawaii and California, there is one of the largest zones of plastic accumulation. It's called the Great Pacific Garbage Patch. This area covers 617,800 square miles (1.6 million square kilometers)—an area twice the size of Texas and three times the size of France. There are four easy steps you can take today to decrease the amount of plastic that reaches the sea:

1. Reduce single-use plastic. You can start by politely saying no to plastic straws at restaurants; you can also use refillable water bottles and bring reusable bags when you and your parents go shopping.

2. Take part in cleanups of your local beaches and rivers.

3. Pick up trash and recyclables, even if they are not yours. It only takes a moment and sets a great example for others.

4. Spread the word! Help others become aware of the problem and let them know how they can become part of the solution.

Rays and Skates

There are over 600 species of rays and skates, including stingrays, electric rays, butterfly rays, round rays, manta rays, guitarfish, and sawfish. These types of fish have flattened bodies with five pairs of gill slits on the underside, rather than on the sides. Their **pectoral fins** look almost like wings and are usually connected to their heads.

Stingray

The stingray has a whip-like tail with a venomous barb for defense. Often buried in soft dirt with only its large eyes uncovered, this species uses specialized openings called spiracles to pump water to its gill cavity.

Giant Manta Ray

With a wingspan of up to 29 feet (8.8 meters), the giant manta ray is the largest ray in the world. Found worldwide, manta rays are **filter feeders** and have been found feeding in shallow waters less than 40 feet (10 meters) or diving after prey to depths exceeding 3,280 feet (1,000 meters).

Sawfish

The sawfish, once found along the whole southeast coast of the United States, is now only found off the coast of Florida. The sawfish feeds by swimming through schools of fish and slashing its chainsaw-like snout called a **rostrum** back and forth to disable prey. It also uses its saw to defend against large predators such as sharks.

Did You Know?

When feeding, manta rays are known to gather in groups called squadrons.

Unlike the other seas of the world, the Sargasso Sea has no land boundaries. Instead, it's defined by the ocean currents that surround it. These boundary currents form the North Atlantic Gyre, one of the world's five major **gyres**. Named for the free-floating patch of seaweed called Sargassum, the Sargasso Sea is a habitat for a variety of marine species, a **spawning** site where animals deposit eggs, and a food source for migrating animals.

Eel

American and European eels fascinate scientists with their life-ending migration to the Sargasso Sea after living 10 to 15 years in freshwater. The adult eels make this single trip in order to spawn. Their **fertilized** eggs hatch, then the eel larvae will drift for one to three years until they reach the coastal rivers, where they will grow to more than 40 inches (1 meter) in length.

Baby Turtle

Off the eastern coast of the United States lies the Gulf Stream, the western boundary of the Sargasso Sea. When newly hatched sea turtles begin their journey out to sea, they catch a ride on the Gulf Stream to their "floating nursery." Here, the hatchlings will spend a year using the seaweed as cover from predators and dining on the plentiful, bite-size morsels.

Sargassum Fish

The sargassum fish camouflages itself among the sargassum and can rapidly change color to match its surroundings. It is a very hungry hunter and feeds by ambush, luring fish close, then lunging forward and swallowing its prey whole.

Made for Speed

With nowhere to hide, a game of cat-and-mouse in the sunlight zone of the open ocean usually ends with the faster swimmer winning. To be fast in this region, fish are rarely found with spines or bulging parts that would slow them down in water. Practically all fish here have streamlined bodies that are muscular, especially the tails. Stiff fins also provide lift at high speeds. With these adaptations for swimming, it is no coincidence that the sunlight zone is home to the ocean's fastest swimmers.

Sailfish

The sailfish is easily recognizable by its sail-like **dorsal fin** that extends the entire length of its body. The sailfish, like sharks and tunas, has a particular arrangement of blood vessels that allows it to keep its body temperature higher than the surrounding water. This lets it move quicker and smarter when hunting in cooler water.

Mako Shark

With top speeds of 45 miles per hour (74 kph), the mako is the fastest shark on the planet. The mako grows exceptionally fast compared to its cousins and boasts a striking coloring, with deep purple upper surfaces, silvery sides, and white underneath.

Did You Know?

The black marlin, clocked at speeds of over 80 mph (129 kph), is the fastest fish in the ocean.

Flying Fish

The flying fish has evolved a special defense when threatened. It begins by using its torpedo-like shape to gain speeds of about 37 miles per hour (60 kph). Angling upward, it rapidly beats its tail to launch itself out of the water and glide through the air to distances of up to 655 feet (200 meters) on its greatly enlarged pectoral fins.

41

A Continuous Game of Hide-and-Seek

I n all its realms, the ocean is a continuous game of hide-and-seek among predators and their prey. What makes it more challenging is that in some areas, there are very few places to hide. Most animals have adapted and use natural tactics to help them detect their prey or take cover from their enemies.

Sense Organs

Fish have good eyesight and a sense organ called a lateral line running lengthwise down their bodies to detect movement in the surrounding water. Many predatory fish—including sharks, tunas, and billfish—also have well-developed hearing. They are strongly attracted to splashes and irregular vibrations, such as those caused by an injured animal.

Camouflage and Countershading

Protective coloring is common among many marine species. Some predators and prey have coloring that hides or camouflages them in their surroundings. Countershading, a coloration where the back is dark and the belly is light, is helpful for animals in the sunlight zone. Looking down, the dark back blends with the blackness of the depths. The light belly blends in with the sunlight when looking up.

Echolocation

A sensory system based on hearing called echolocation is used by all toothed whales. Echolocation helps an animal find prey and become familiar with new surroundings. These marine mammals echolocate by sending bursts of sound waves, or sharp clicks, through the water. The reflected echoes tell how far away an animal or object is.

Did You Know?

The giant squid has the largest eyes ever documented. Up to 10 inches (25 centimeters) in diameter, these peepers are the size of dinner plates!

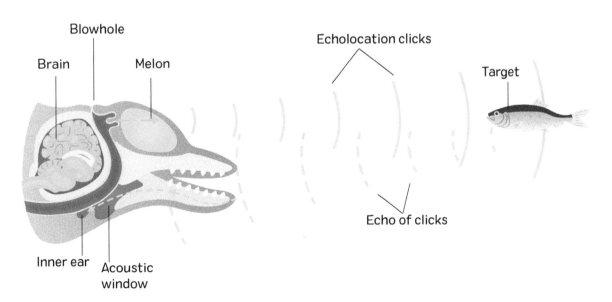

CHAPTER 2
Kelp Forests

Marine Forests

A kelp forest is a large, dense patch of kelp where fronds create a thick mat floating along the surface called a canopy. This underwater habitat is home to thousands of invertebrates, crustaceans, fishes, marine mammals, a few sharks, and seabirds. Kelp grows vertically toward the sunlight, with taller organisms shading the smaller ones. New growth occurs when a larger species dies and allows enough sunlight to penetrate to the bottom. Because the kelp relies on sunlight, it is always found in coastal waters. It reaches its full growth in one to two years.

Basic Kelp Structure

Kelp is greenish-brown in color and has a stem-like structure that can grow up to 150 feet (46 meters). It has many leaf-like blades shaped like swords. These make food from sunlight using **photosynthesis**. Underneath the blades are "bladders," or gas-filled balls that help the kelp stay upright. This allows the blades to get the most sunlight. Kelp secures itself to the rocky bottom using "anchors" called holdfasts.

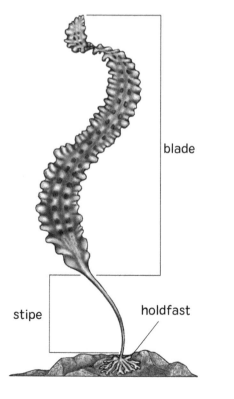

blade

stipe

holdfast

Trophic Process

Kelp forests support many food webs. The food webs consist of steps, or **trophic levels**, that energy passes through. Animals that feed directly on the kelp are **primary consumers**, such as sea urchins, snails, and crabs. The level above that is **secondary consumers**, like fish and sea stars. Above that are **tertiary consumers**, and so on until a top predator like a sea otter or shark finishes a food web.

Giant Kelp

Giant kelp is the planet's largest bottom-dwelling organism, growing as much as 2 feet (0.6 meters) a day until it reaches heights up to 150 feet (46 meters). Giant kelp has a chemical called **algin**, which is used in many everyday items. Algin has a special property that makes ice cream remain thick, medicine tablets stick together, and lipstick stay on lips.

Highly Productive Ecosystem

Kelp forests are found along 25 percent of the world's coastlines, creating habitats for a great diversity of species. Kelp grows remarkably fast and plays a vital role in removing carbon dioxide from the atmosphere through photosynthesis. Scientists have found that kelp ecosystems can eliminate up to 20 times more carbon dioxide per acre than land forests.

Sea Kelp vs. Seaweed: Is There A Difference?

No. Kelp *is* a seaweed. Seaweed is a type of marine algae. It is not a true plant because it doesn't have leaves, stems, and roots. Seaweed comes in many forms and three colors—green, red, and brown. Kelp is the most complex and largest of all brown algae.

Buffet for Birds

Floating fronds of kelp create a canopy that is characteristic of kelp forests. Below the canopy is a rich and diverse ecosystem full of fish, marine worms called **polychaetes**, snails, bivalves, and crustaceans. This assortment of marine life is a dinner buffet for seabirds that come to graze.

Gull

Gulls are predators and scavengers, happy to eat just about anything. The same goes for the kelp gull, which gets its common name from its habit of feeding in kelp forests. They will often steal food from other predators rather than hunting themselves. Gulls have few natural predators but when floating on the surface, they are sometimes eaten by sharks.

Snowy Egret

Once hunted for its long, snowy white feathers, the snowy egret made a rapid recovery after protection measures were put in place. The snowy egret feeds while walking, running, or even hovering, striking prey with its long, sharp bill.

Great Blue Heron

The great blue heron doesn't hunt like the snowy egret. Instead, it sits on floating kelp, waiting for its meal to swim by. When it does, the blue heron will strike with lightning-quick speed to grab a fish or crab. Despite its impressive size—sometimes growing as tall as a 10-year-old child with a wingspan of over 6 feet (1.8 m)—the great blue heron weighs only about 5 pounds.

Cormorant

Cormorants can be easily identified by the fact that they float low in the water with only their neck above the surface. They feed alone underwater, diving after crabs, worms, and small fish to depths of 150 feet (45 meters). This makes cormorants some of the deepest-diving birds around.

A Delicate Balance

Kelp forests form a complex environment for animals that go there to feed. Animals of the kelp forest do not feed on the actively growing kelp, but they do eat the drift kelp that breaks loose and eventually sinks to the bottom or washes to shore. The kelp ecosystem is dependent on a particular species called the **keystone species**—the sea otter—which keeps the ecosystem from collapsing. One of the sea otter's favorite delicacies is the sea urchin, which loves kelp.

Sea Otter

The sea otter was nearly hunted out of existence for its fur in the early 20th century. When that happened, not only did the kelp beds disappear, but so did the marine life that depended on the kelp. When conservationists moved some otters back to an ecosystem where kelp once thrived, the sea otters' numbers grew, sea urchins declined, and the kelp began to grow again.

Sea Otter

Size/Weight	3.3 to 5 ft (1 to 1.5 m) / 30 to 100 lbs (13 to 45 kg)
Diet	sea urchins, abalones, clams, mussels, and snails
Speed	5 mph (8 kph)
Status	endangered
Life Span	10 to 20 years

Did You Know?

Sea otters have the thickest fur of any animal, with 600,000 to 1 million hair follicles per square inch!

Sea Urchin

The sea urchin is an essential grazer in the kelp communities, feeding on drift kelp. Unfortunately, sea urchin populations sometimes grow too large, allowing them to feed on the holdfasts of kelp and breaking them loose. What is left are "urchin deserts," where large areas of kelp are completely cleared away. But when the sea urchin's predator, the sea otter, is present, urchins hide in crevices and only eat the scraps of kelp that drift away.

Safe Haven

Kelp forests provide shelter for numerous marine organisms. Whether it's a safe feeding ground for hatchlings or a place to hide from roaming predators and storm surges, the dense kelp's protection is useful for survival.

Shelter from the Storm

When storms hit coastal areas, bringing high winds and rough seas, larger marine life like seabirds and mammals take shelter in the kelp forests. The dense canopy and countless blades of the stalks help weaken currents and waves.

Nurseries

The slow currents and warmer surface temperatures created by the dense canopy of the kelp forest make a perfect nursery for many marine organisms. Small fish, birds, and even whales use the thick mat of blades as a safe shelter for their young from predators and rough seas.

Protection from Predators

On occasion, gray whales have been spotted in kelp forests, eating the invertebrates and crustaceans found there. The gray whales will also use the dim cover of the dense canopy to hide from predatory killer whales.

On the rocky floor of kelp forests live giant green sea anemones. These massive cnidarians have a helpful relationship with algae. Algae need sunlight for photosynthesis, a process in which they use sunlight to make food for themselves. The anemone receives some of the nutrients that the algae make from photosynthesis, and in return the algae get a place to live.

Kelp Forest Fish

Fish are extremely common in kelp communities, feeding and taking shelter in all layers. Some species are bottom feeders, while others feed in the kelp columns. Because ocean temperatures are shifting due to climate change, kelp forests may see new inhabitants as fish from coral reefs move into this more temperate habitat.

California Sheephead

The California sheephead can grow to 3 feet (0.9 meters) in length and does something incredible when it is about eight years old—the females turn into males. This biological transformation takes about a year. The sheephead actively hunts during the day but will find a cave or crevice to rest in at night.

Did You Know?

To protect itself from predators at night, the California sheephead will encase itself in a mucus cocoon to mask its scent.

Giant Kelpfish

The body of a giant kelpfish is long and shaped like a kelp blade, making the kelp forest a perfect habitat to blend into. Like seaweed, giant kelpfish can also be red, green, and brown—and can change colors to match their surroundings.

Garibaldi

The bright orange garibaldi is highly territorial and fiercely protective, especially when guarding a nest of eggs. Male garibaldis are responsible for raising the young after they hatch, and will chase down much larger fish and even scuba divers if they come too close.

Weedy Seadragon

The weedy seadragons of Australia are not good swimmers, so they sway with the currents like the seaweed that makes up their habitat. Unlike a male seahorse that has a pouch to carry eggs, the male seadragon's eggs are attached to the underside of its tail.

Impact of Unsustainable Fishing

What We Can Do About It?

If a fish population is going to last, or be sustainable, the number of fish caught can be no more than the number of new young added. Unfortunately, commercial overfishing has become the biggest threat for fish species. Around 90 percent of the biggest fishes in the world are already gone. Sharks, which are slow to grow and reproduce, have critically declined in parts of the world. You and your family can help by buying sustainable seafood. Use online and up-to-date national guides to learn what seafood choices are the best and which should be avoided for now. Consumer guides can be found online or downloaded at SeafoodWatch.org.

Pinnipeds of the Kelp Forest

Pinnipeds are a group of mammals that have paddle-shaped flippers for swimming, but still need to rest and breed on land. This includes the sea lions, harbor seals, elephant seals, and fur seals often found feeding on the fish and escaping predators in kelp forests.

Harbor Seal

Unlike most pinnipeds, harbor seals rarely interact with others. They may haul out of the water in groups, but they usually do not touch one another. They are the least vocal of the seals, but if touched, they will growl, snort, scratch, or even bite.

Harbor Seal

Size/Weight	6 ft (1.85 m) / 370 lb (168 kg)
Diet	squids, crustaceans, mollusks, and fishes
Speed	12 mph (19 kph)
Status	least concern
Life Span	20 to 35 years

Did You Know?

The elephant seal is the deepest-diving pinniped, reaching depths of over 5,000 feet (1,524 meters) in search of food!

Elephant Seal

The elephant seal spends 80 percent of its life at sea, covering long distances in search of food. It only comes ashore to mate, rest, or molt. The Piedras Blancas Elephant Seal Rookery, off the coast of California, is a perfect stretch of land with wide beaches, offering pups protection from high water. The giant kelp forest sitting off its coast also protects elephant seals and their pups from predators.

Fur Seal

More closely related to sea lions than true seals, the fur seal has the ability to walk on all four flippers and has external ears. Fur seals have fine, thick fur, with 300,000 hairs per square inch, making them targets for hunters who nearly made them extinct. Protection laws are now in place, and many groups have made a comeback.

Jeweled Invertebrates

The most commonly found invertebrates—animals without a backbone—in a kelp forest are bristle worms, prawns, snails, and brittle stars. But some of these are so remarkable in color and uniqueness that these jewels of the sea deserve a spotlight.

Purple-Ring Topsnail

If the weather is good in the kelp forest, this snail climbs the vertical stalks toward the sun. The purple-ring topsnail can be spotted by its pinkish body and colorful shell that features bright purple bands, contrasting starkly with the rest of the orange-yellow shell.

Sunflower Star

Size/Weight	39 in (99 cm) / up to 13.4 lb (5 kg)
Diet	sea urchins, clams, crabs, and sand dollars
Speed	40 ipm (1 m/s)
Status	endangered
Life Span	3 to 5 years

Sunflower Star

The sunflower star has soft skin that showcases a range of colors. But what makes this magnificent creature stand out from other sea stars is its arrangement of 24 arms, each with 15,000 tube feet. The unique adaptation lets this predator hunt for food at remarkable speeds of over 40 inches (1 meter) per minute.

Nudibranch

The most striking of the kelp forest animals is the nudibranch. This sea slug lacks a shell, making it easy to see its decorative colors and patterns, which serve as a warning to predators of its toxic taste. In one patch of kelp, you may see purple nudibranchs with orange gills or blue ones with yellow polka dots.

Night Hunters

Once the sun sets and it gets dark, many marine animals will find a crevice or holdfast to rest in for the night. But to other animals of the kelp forest, the darkness is where they have the best advantage. Many **nocturnal** animals have common characteristics such as a red or brown color. These are the first colors that become difficult to see when the light fades. These creatures tend to be carnivorous, using the night as a perfect time to hunt.

Bat Ray

Size/Weight	4 to 6 ft (1.2 to 1.85 m) / up to 200 lbs (90 kg)
Diet	mollusks, crustaceans, and small fishes
Speed	unknown
Status	least concern
Life Span	23 years

Bat Ray

During the day, the bat ray rests on the seafloor of deeper, cooler waters far from shore. But come night, it moves into kelp beds and begins to search for prey. The bat ray will rapidly flap its long pectoral fins that resemble bat wings to move sand and expose hidden shrimp, crabs, clams, and small bony fish.

Giant Pacific Octopus

The giant Pacific octopus is the largest octopus species, at 30 feet (9 meters) across. With its reddish-brown color, you would think this creature would be easy to spot among the kelp forest. However, it uses specialized cells in its skin to change colors and textures, allowing it to blend in with rocky outcroppings and stalks of kelp.

Did You Know?

Another night hunter of the kelp forest, the horn shark, eats so many purple urchins that its teeth are stained purple!

Leopard Shark

Averaging about 6 feet (1.8 meters) in length, the leopard shark has a tan body with dark brown bars, saddles, and spots on its back and side. Using the cover of night, leopard sharks quietly hunt along the bottom of kelp beds, searching for crabs, clams, fish, and their eggs to eat.

CHAPTER 3

Coastlines and Shorelines

We're most familiar with ocean life along the coasts—you don't need a boat, or even snorkel gear, to observe and learn about this environment. Scientists can study organisms without expensive equipment, and they can return to the same location again and again.

What creatures can you find here? It depends on the bottom of the ecosystem. Some organisms have adapted to soft, sandy bottoms, which are very different from the sharp, rocky shores other plants and animals prefer.

Sandy Shores

In the **intertidal zone** of sandy beaches, areas that are underwater at high tide become dry and bare at low tide. Animals in this habitat are never found in the same spot—they must move to follow the fall and rise of the water levels. Most animals burrow or dig a tunnel in the sand for protection and to keep from being washed away.

Wrack

Anytime you walk along a sandy beach, you probably notice clumps of seaweed, surf grass, and kelp that have washed up from the ocean. This is called wrack. Because plants and seaweed can't grow in the shifting beach sands, wrack is the main food source for many sand-dwelling animals, which in turn feed a variety of shorebirds.

Razor Clam

Deep in the sand of surf-swept beaches are razor clams. If a predator, such as a clam worm, attacks from below, a razor clam escapes by using its strong muscular foot to push itself out of its hole. If the attack comes from above, the razor clam can dig as fast as a foot per minute, quickly escaping danger.

Bloodworm

The bloodworm, named for its red color, can be found in the damp sand of the intertidal zone during low tide. Being poor swimmers, bloodworms burrow into the sand, leaving tiny holes behind. These worms prey on small crustaceans and other worms with a powerful, venomous bite.

Beach-Spawning Fish

To help their young survive, beach-spawning fish use high tide to reach the uppermost portions of the sand to lay and fertilize their eggs. They also might use the waves to scatter their eggs high on the beach away from predators. The highest tides, called the **semilunar tides**, occur twice a month around the full and new moon. Eggs hatch during these tides so that the young fish can swim away.

Grunion

In early spring, thousands of grunions emerge from the ocean, riding waves of the high tide onto California's shores. Females dig into the soft sand tail-first to release their eggs, while the males wrap around them and fertilize the eggs. When the next set of waves rolls up, the grunion ride it back to the ocean, leaving their eggs buried in the sand.

Grass Puffer

The grass puffer will ride the high tide in, stranding itself among pebble beaches and waiting for the return ride back to sea, where the fish spawn in the shallower water. The fertilized eggs are then scattered high on the beach by waves until the next high tide. Then they hatch and the babies return to the ocean.

Mummichog

The mummichog is a small fish that spawns near the water's edge in areas where there is little wave action. Fertilized eggs are placed in empty seashells or on plants to protect them for the next 9 to 12 days. There they wait to hatch, with the young returning to sea on the semilunar high tide.

Shore Crabs

Shore crabs come in a variety of species and have a big impact along coasts and on beaches. Many are **omnivorous**, meaning that they eat other animal species along with plants and seeds. Crabs are scavengers that dine on rotting material, recycling energy back into the ecosystem. Shore crabs also play an important part in the marine food chain. Many are a source of food for other animals, such as marine birds and larger crabs.

Ghost Crab

The ghost crab, named for its see-through shell, comes out of its burrow at night to feed on loggerhead sea turtle eggs, insects, clams, and sand crabs. While some crabs need to return to water periodically to wet their gills, the ghost crab can stay on land, using tiny hairs on the bottom of its legs to suck up water from the damp sand.

Ghost Crab

Size/Weight	1.5 to 2 in (3.75 to 5 cm) / unknown
Diet	insects, filter feeders, turtle eggs, and scavenged food
Speed	6 fps (1.8 m/s)
Status	least concern
Life Span	3 years

Did You Know?

Ghost crabs use "teeth" in their stomach called a gastric mill to produce a growling sound when danger nears.

Fiddler Crab

With its distinctive giant claw, the fiddler crab builds burrows up to 2 feet deep. These burrows are precious to fiddler crabs, which are never more than 3 to 6 feet (1 to 2 meters) from the entrance. When a fiddler crab leaves the safety of its burrow, its biggest threat is larger crabs looking to steal its home. When this occurs, a male fiddler will use its giant claws to fight.

Sand Crab

If you scooped up a handful of wet sand at the beach, you would probably pick up some sand crabs, too. Also known as the mole crab, this 1.5-inch-long (3.8 centimeters) critter lives in the wet shoreline sand searching for food. Unlike most crabs, it does not have claws. Instead, it uses its feathery antennae as a screen to catch plankton.

Burrowing in the Sand

Crabs use their five pairs of legs to burrow in the sand, avoiding predators and creating a safe place for their eggs. Most crabs have hard shells, but many shed their **exoskeletons** as they grow, making them vulnerable during their short soft-shell period. Baby crabs are also vulnerable when they hatch, so burrows give them protection when they first emerge from the egg.

Mangrove Forests

Mangroves grow in the tropics along coastal intertidal zones. They have adapted to living in saltwater and are recognized by their tangle of interlocking roots that make the trees appear to be standing on stilts above the water. These trees are vital to coastal ecosystems. Not only do they reduce **erosion** from waves, tides, and storm surges, they also provide a habitat for many species. Mangrove forests have been rapidly disappearing due to the coastal development of shrimp farms, golf courses, and roads. They are now considered an endangered ecosystem.

Saltwater Crocodiles

The saltwater crocodile is the largest reptile on the planet, reaching lengths of more than 23 feet (6.5 meters) and weighing over 2,200 pounds (1,000 kilograms). It can hold its breath for a long time, and uses stealth and its size to lunge and attack large land mammals and birds. These cold-blooded animals only leave the water to warm up in the sun.

Mudskipper

The mudskipper is a small fish that spends about half of its life on land, sometimes going a week without getting in the water. Tiny chambers outside of its gills trap water, allowing it to perform this feat. Large protruding eyes on top of its head are adapted to see on land and can be remoistened in water-filled "cups" below its eyes.

Did You Know?

The saltwater crocodile has the most powerful bite in the world, almost 25 times more powerful than an average human's bite!

Lemon Shark

With their shallow waters, mangrove forests offer less danger than the open sea and coral reefs. Some animals, like the lemon shark, have learned to take advantage and use this protected area for breeding and giving birth to their young. The pups will remain for one to four years to feed on small fish and crustaceans until they are old enough to head to deeper waters.

Crown-of-Thorns Starfish

The nocturnal crown-of-thorns starfish moves through the reef feeding on coral. It helps the coral diversity by eating faster-growing coral, giving the slow growers time to catch up. However, when the crown-of-thorns starfish population explodes due to an increase in nutrients from pollution, the impact of these eager eaters can be disastrous.

Rocky Shores

Life on the rocky shores is tough. They are usually located on steep coasts without much mud or sand, and organisms that thrive here deal with the constant pounding of waves, regular exposure to the sun and air, and hungry predators. This results in organisms forming zones at different heights: the upper, middle, and lower intertidal zones. Because there is not much sediment, most rocky shore animals are filter feeders, meaning they have to be covered by water to filter the small organisms from it. But the main problem is space, which is so limited that often organisms attach to one another instead of the rocks.

Upper Intertidal Zone

The upper intertidal zone lies above the high tide line. With few marine predators, large numbers of periwinkles and limpets graze on algae here. These marine snails use a structure of tiny teeth called a radula to scrape the algae off the rocks. A snail's muscular foot forms a tight bond to the rocks, making it difficult for predators to pry it off.

Middle Intertidal Zone

The middle intertidal zone is regularly submerged at high tide, then exposed to air at low tide. Acorn barnacles and rock barnacles almost always inhabit the upper portion, while mussels and gooseneck barnacles dominate the lower part. Barnacles are related to crabs and shrimp and secrete a natural "glue" that cements them to rocks, other sea life, and the undersides of boats.

Lower Intertidal Zone

Since this zone is underwater most of the time, it is dominated by seaweeds. This thick blanket of algae is important to grazers and is home to another species of periwinkle. Other small animals hide from predators among the seaweed, including sea urchins, worms, and sea slugs.

Tide Pools

Intertidal organisms have two ways to survive when the tide goes out and leaves them exposed to air—they can close up like barnacles and mussels do to prevent water loss, or they can move and hide somewhere wet until the tide comes back in. The perfect place to stay wet is in tide pools—small and large spaces in rocks that hold water after the tide goes out.

Hermit Crab

The hermit crab is a small crustacean commonly found in tide pools. Because it doesn't have a shell, the hermit crab needs to find a way to protect its soft **abdomen**. It does this by finding a shell that has been discarded by another animal, such as a periwinkle. As hermit crabs grow, they need to find larger shells to "borrow" until they become full-size adults.

Sea Squirt

The sea squirt, named for its tendency to squirt water when touched, is a species of marine life called **tunicates**. The sea squirt attaches to rocky surfaces, protected by a gel-like covering called a **tunic**. Some sea squirts are **invasive species** in many coastal ecosystems. With no known predators, they reproduce rapidly, taking resources from other species and making the seafloor uninhabitable for fish eggs and shellfish larvae.

Sea Anemone

Tide pool sea anemones tend to live in larger colonies that are packed tightly together. Just like jellyfish, sea anemones have tentacles covered with specialized stinging cells called nematocysts, which contain a venomous barb. The **venom** will paralyze prey so that the anemone can slowly pull the prey into its mouth.

Sculpin

Sculpins hide in the seaweed and rocks of tide pools with the help of camouflage. Their coloring makes it hard for larger fish and hungry shorebirds to find them. Sculpins use the tides to help them hunt. They follow the tide in to hunt in higher pools, then follow the tide back out to the lower pools.

Seagrass Meadows

Several species of seagrasses grow in water to form thick, rich meadows. Seagrasses have leaves, roots, flowers, and seeds like **terrestrial** plants, but need water to support their blades because they do not have stems. Seagrasses are the primary **producers** of the ocean, making their own food through photosynthesis. Marine **herbivores**, such as sea turtles, manatees, and sea urchins, come to graze on the seagrass. When it dies, it forms **detritus**, which is fed upon by sea cucumbers and clams.

Pistol Shrimp

Pistol shrimp have a large claw that produces a distinctive snapping sound, which may give this 2-inch animal the title of "the loudest animal in the ocean." This sound is louder than a gunshot and can actually break glass, making it difficult to keep the pistol shrimp in aquariums. The snap causes a shock-wave bubble that stuns or even kills its prey.

Seahorse

Seahorses, named for their heads that resemble horses, are tiny fish that have special skin cells that change color to blend in with their surroundings. They are among the few fish that swim upright, although not very well. To make sure they don't get swept away by currents, they wind their tails around seagrass to help anchor them.

Did You Know?

Seahorses and their close relatives, seadragons, are the only species in which the males carry the young and give birth!

Coastal Pollution

What We Can Do About It

More than 80 percent of coastal and marine pollution comes from land. One of the biggest sources is **nonpoint source pollution**, a combination of pollutants rather than one identifiable source. Nonpoint source pollution comes from oil residue washed off streets, soil lost from construction sites, and stormwater **runoff**, which is water emptied into streams and rivers that may contain fertilizers or pesticides. To help reduce coastal pollution, you can do the following:

1. Participate in stream cleanup programs.

2. Clean up after your pets. Their waste may contain harmful organisms that could affect marine life.

3. Encourage your family to save gas by walking or biking to school or the store.

4. Don't dump anything down storm drains.

Manatees

Once mistaken by sailors for mythical mermaids, these gentle marine mammals are usually found grazing on seagrass for 6 to 8 hours a day. This large, slow-moving animal uses its flat, paddle-shaped tail and two flippers to move around in the shallow waters it inhabits. When water temperature drops, manatees will move to warmer waters, even traveling up rivers to freshwater springs.

Manatees

Size/Weight	8 to 13 ft (2.4 to 4 m) / 440 to 1,300 lb (200 to 590 kg)
Diet	herbivore
Speed	5 mph (8 kph), with short bursts to 15 mph (24 kph)
Status	vulnerable
Life Span	40 years

Making a Comeback

Manatees need to come to the surface for air every 3 to 5 minutes, so they stay in shallow waters. In the past, they were vulnerable to motorboat accidents, fishing nets, and crowded waters, putting them on the endangered species list in 1967. In 1973, laws were put in place making it illegal to bother, feed, or harm manatees. Speed zones for boats were also added where manatees live or travel regularly. Now, decades later, manatee numbers have grown. Manatees are no longer considered endangered.

Did You Know?

Manatees and dugongs are not related to dolphins and whales. They are related to elephants!

Dugong

The dugong is closely related to manatees. Both are affectionately called "sea cows" due to their slow nature and grass-eating tendencies. However, unlike manatees, the dugong has a fluked tail, bristles instead of whiskers, and a longer life span of 70 years compared to manatees' 40 years.

CHAPTER 4
Coral Reefs

Coral Reefs

Coral reefs are often called the rain forests of the ocean. Not only do coral reefs provide shelter, food, and nurseries for about 25 percent of the ocean's fish, but they also support invertebrates, plants, birds, sea turtles, and marine mammals. Three main types of coral reef exist—**fringing reefs**, **barrier reefs**, and **atolls**. Fringing reefs are the most common and grow in a narrow band close to the shore. Barrier reefs occur a little farther from shore than fringing reefs. Both protect coastlines from storms and erosion. Atolls are rings of reef with steep outer slopes that enclose a lagoon.

The Great Barrier Reef:
The World's Largest Coral Reef

Stretching more than 1,200 miles (2,000 km), the Great Barrier Reef sits off the coast of Queensland, Australia, and is the largest living organism on Earth. It's so big, in fact, that it is visible from space! While thousands of species inhabit the Great Barrier Reef, only a few are reef-building organisms. Coral reefs are made of huge amounts of calcium carbonate, known as limestone, which are actually skeletons of coral built up over time.

Hard Coral

Often mistaken for rocks, hard corals are the main reef-building animals. Corals are colonies of many **polyps** that produce limestone skeletons. These tiny polyps look a lot like sea anemones and use their tentacles to capture food. Together, the colony forms a thin living tissue layer on the surface. As polyps die, they become hard, leaving a coral skeleton that forms the reef's framework.

Teamwork on the Reef

Nearly all reef-building corals contain **zooxanthellae** (pronounced zow-uh-zan-THEH-lai), algae that live in the coral's tissue that can make their own food through photosynthesis. Zooxanthellae help the coral in two ways: They convert sunlight into nourishment for the host coral, and they help glue its skeleton so they can safely stay in one place.

Soft Coral

While soft corals are not reef builders, they make up almost half of the reef. Because they don't have a limestone skeleton, they can grow faster than hard corals. Many soft corals contain sharp needles called **sclerites** that keep predators from feeding on them. Soft corals include the sea fan, encrusting gorgonian, and sea fingers, which grow into wide, finger-like stalks.

Sponges

Sponges live permanently attached to the bottom of the ocean floor or to some hard surface. They have simple body plans and no tissues or organs, but they do have specialized cells that carry out specific functions, such as capturing food and regenerating. With approximately 9,000 species known, sponges come in a variety of shapes, colors, and sizes. However, all share a feature of having tiny holes, or **pores**, on their surface for water flow and feeding.

Boring Sponge

The boring sponge can be recognized by its bright yellow and orange color, sometimes covering an area of several square feet. The boring sponge gets its name from its behavior of boring, or piercing a hole into mollusk shells and coral skeletons in order to hold itself in place. Unfortunately, this habit eventually kills the organism it clings to.

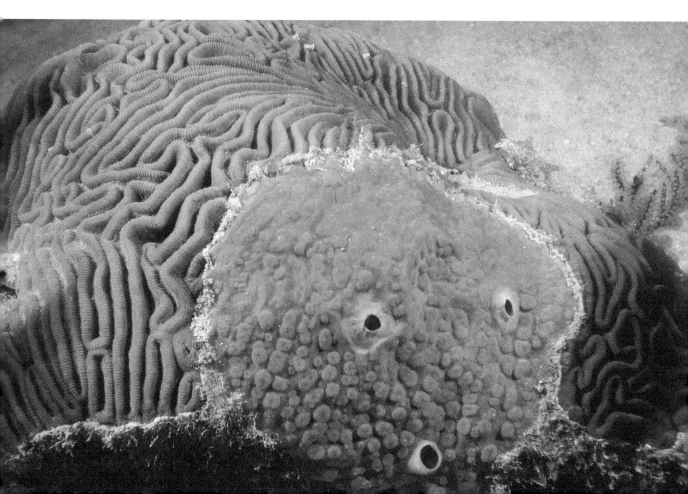

Coralline Sponge

Once known only as fossils, living specimens of coralline sponges, or sclerosponges, were discovered in underwater caves and on steep coral reef slopes. Coralline sponges resemble coral because they form a calcium carbonate skeleton beneath their body, helping support the coral reef framework in some areas.

Coral Bleaching

When oceans become too warm or too polluted, it can cause stress to organisms. When these conditions upset coral, they can kick out the zooxanthellae living in their cells and turn completely white. This is known as **coral bleaching**. Bleached coral will not grow, and its structure becomes weak. If temperatures return to normal and the pollutant is removed, coral can recover with the help of new zooxanthellae moving in, or those left behind restoring their numbers. Unfortunately, if the stressful situation continues, the coral will die and the organisms living around the reef will lose their habitat. We can all do our part to help prevent coral bleaching, such as:

1. Look for sunscreens labeled "Reef Safe" or "No Oxybenzone." Cut down on sunscreen by wearing long-sleeved shirts and rash guards—but be sure to cover any exposed skin with sunscreen!

2. Avoid touching or coming in contact with coral—it can damage and sometimes even kill these fragile animals.

3. Share these ideas with friends and family to help protect this fragile ecosystem.

Reef Fish

Reef fish live among or close to coral reefs and are critical to the health of the reef ecosystem. The main benefit reef fish provide for coral is eating the algae competing for space on the bottom of the reef. If left unchecked, algae will overgrow and shade coral, eventually killing them. By devouring these algae, reef fish do not allow them to grow out of control, and this vital ecosystem is preserved.

Giant Grouper

The largest of all reef-dwelling bony fish, the giant grouper can grow up to 8.9 feet (2.7 meters) in length and top the scales at over 650 pounds (300 kilograms)! When unsuspecting prey pass a hungry grouper, it creates a powerful suction, opening its mouth and sucking in fish, juvenile turtles, and even small sharks, which it swallows whole.

Parrotfish

One of the most important fish on coral reefs is the colorful and always hungry parrotfish. It spends up to 90 percent of its day eating! The parrotfish bites and scrapes off algae that would otherwise smother healthy coral.

Lionfish

Once only found in the Indo-Pacific region, the lionfish is now an invasive species in the Atlantic. It preys on over 50 species of fish, ambushing its prey by using its large, fan-like pectoral fins to corner them. With no known predator in the Atlantic reef, the lionfish is killing off helpful species of fish that keep algae from smothering the coral.

Pufferfish

Pufferfish, when threatened, can expand to 2 to 3 times their normal size by swallowing huge amounts of water. Some species of pufferfish will expose sharp spines containing strong toxins that can kill predators. When ready to mate, male pufferfish will spend seven to nine days constructing intricate patterns in the sand to attract females.

Maori Wrasse

The Maori wrasse, also known as a humphead wrasse, is an enormous reef fish, growing over 6 feet long. As protector of the reef, the Maori wrasse eats sea hares, boxfish, and even crown-of-thorns starfish that attack the reef.

Symbiotic Relationship

On the coral reef, it is common to find two organisms of different species forming a **symbiotic relationship**, where two animals live together and at least one of them benefits. Sometimes, in the case of **commensalism**, one organism will benefit, while the other feels no effects at all. This is different from **parasitism**, where one organism benefits while the other is harmed and sometimes even killed. **Mutualism** is where both organisms benefit from the relationship, with many examples found on the coral reef.

Clown Fish and Sea Anemones

Since it's able to withstand the sea anemone's stinging tentacles, the clown fish uses the sea anemone for protection from predators. While living among the tentacles, the clown fish keeps them clean from parasites and chases away butterfly fish that come to feed on the anemone.

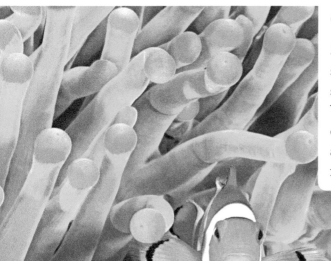

Giant Clams and Algae

Like most clams, the giant clam filter feeds small prey from the water that **siphons** through its body. In the case of the giant clam, algae living on the clam's shell also receive nutrients from this feeding. In return, the photosynthetic algae convert sunlight to energy for both themselves and the giant clam.

Christmas Tree Worms and Coral

The Christmas tree worm lives up to 40 years in once place. It usually finds a home by boring or piercing into the hard skeleton of coral. In return, it protects its coral home from predators such as the crown-of-thorns starfish, which has been known to devastate entire coral reef colonies.

Green sea turtles will present themselves to a swarm of yellow tangs, which immediately start scraping and eating the algae from the turtle's body. This mutualistic relationship helps keep the green sea turtles healthy while providing a meal for the fish.

Sea Turtles

All species of sea turtle are keystone species, feeding on jellyfish and seagrass. Sea turtles migrate from feeding sites to nesting grounds on sandy beaches. Females will leave a clutch of 100 to 200 eggs in a nest, cover it with sand, then return to the ocean. The most dangerous time for a sea turtle is when it's a hatchling and must make its way from the nest to the sea.

While migrating, sea turtles help other organisms by either providing a habitat for "hitchhikers" like barnacles and **remoras** or acting as an umbrella for fish, sheltering them from predators.

Green Sea Turtle

Among the largest of the sea turtles, the green sea turtle is the only herbivore of the species. It primarily eats seagrasses, acting as a lawnmower to help keep seagrass beds healthy. Juvenile green sea turtles eat seagrass but will also eat crabs, jellyfish, and sponges.

Green Sea Turtle

Size/Weight	up to 5 ft (1.5 m) / up to 700 lbs (320 kg)
Diet	seagrass
Speed	35 mph (56 kph)
Status	endangered
Life Span	> 80 years

Hawksbill Sea Turtle

The hawksbill sea turtle, named for its pointed beak, specializes in eating sea sponges. Without the hawksbill, the sponges would overgrow, suffocating slow-growing corals on the reef. These medium-size turtles have a beautiful shell with a top of golden brown, orange, red, and black, and a light yellow bottom.

Loggerhead Sea Turtle

The loggerhead is found worldwide, but most populations live in Atlantic coastal waters. The loggerhead is a **carnivore**, feeding on hard-shell prey such as whelks and conches. Its powerful jaw muscles, designed to crush prey, are supported by its relatively large head, hence the name.

Leatherback Sea Turtle

The leatherback is the largest turtle in the world, weighing up to 2,200 pounds! It is named for its tough, leathery skin and is the only sea turtle that does not have a hard shell or scales. Unable to crush prey like some of its cousins, it likes to eat soft-bodied animals such as jellyfish and salp, a barrel-shaped organism that drifts in the ocean and resembles a jellyfish. It's mouth and throat are lined with backward-pointing spines to help grip onto slippery jellyfish as it eats.

You Can Help Protect Sea Turtles

Worldwide, six out of seven species of sea turtle are classified as threatened or endangered. Unfortunately, humans hurt sea turtles directly by illegally hunting them for their meat, eggs, and shells. Indirectly, sea turtle populations are dropping due to nesting sites being turned into resorts and public beaches. Sea turtle deaths also occur from getting tangled in fishing gear and choking on plastic garbage. Although these threats seem almost too big to overcome, there are still many things in your control that can help sea turtle conservation. You can:

1. Reduce your use of single-use plastic like straws, plastic bottles, and plastic bags.

2. Participate in beach and coastal cleanups.

3. Avoid releasing balloons at celebrations—they'll most likely end up in the ocean, where turtles can mistake them for food.

4. After leaving the beach, knock down sandcastles and fill in holes, which may become obstacles for nesting turtles or emerging hatchlings.

5. Talk to others about how they can also help save the sea turtles.

Octopuses

Considered by many biologists to be the most intelligent animals, octopuses are curious and resourceful. Easily recognizable with their round bodies and eight long arms, octopuses can be found in all of the world's oceans, with most species found in warm, tropical waters. Octopuses can not only change their skin color for both camouflage and communication, but they can also change their skin's texture to help them blend into their surroundings.

Blue-Ringed Octopus

One of the most dangerous animals in the ocean is the blue-ringed octopus. It has enough powerful venom to kill 26 people within minutes. To hunt, the blue-ringed octopus either releases a cloud of venom into the water, which enters the gills of its prey, or bites and injects venom directly into the wound, immediately paralyzing its prey.

Blue-Ringed Octopus

Size/Weight	5 to 8 in (12 to 20 cm) / 0.22 lbs (10 to 100 g)
Diet	crustaceans and fish
Speed	unknown
Status	least concern
Life Span	2 years

Blanket Octopus

The male blanket octopus grows to about the size of a walnut (0.9 inches [2.5 centimeters]), while the female blanket octopus can grow to an amazing 6 feet long (1.8 meters). This is one of the largest size differences in the same species in the animal kingdom. The female also uses blanket-like webs extending down its arms to help appear larger to potential predators.

The Red Sea Coral Reef

The Red Sea, located between Africa and Asia, is an extension of the Indian Ocean known for its white sand beaches and pristine coral reefs. The Red Sea coral reef is a fringing reef with an impressive length of 2,500 miles (4,000 kilometers). Scientists have been studying the Red Sea because its coral seems to do extremely well in warmer water temperatures. Findings from this research may help protect other coral reefs around the world as they face rising ocean temperatures.

Red Sea Pipefish

Pipefish are related to seahorses and seadragons. Like them, pipefish have elongated snouts. However, their body shape more resembles that of a small eel, as pipefish have no spines. Pipefish are masters of camouflage, using their bright colors and patterns to blend into their surroundings.

Red Sea Flasher Wrasse

With its characteristic eight blue horizontal lines that run the length of its body, the Red Sea flasher wrasse is stunning. As a young fish, this wrasse is pink and blue but changes to orange and red as it matures into an adult.

Giant Moray Eel

The giant moray eel hunts at night, sometimes working with a partner—a coral grouper. The eel swims into crevices, startling fish from their hiding spots into the mouth of a hungry grouper. In return, the grouper uses its size to scare fish toward the reef, where the eel waits and ambushes them.

Artificial Reefs

Sometimes, coral reefs that have been destroyed by pollution or development need help recovering. One strategy is to build **artificial reefs** to help boost biodiversity in a depleted area. Artificial reefs can be human-made structures built in a specific underwater location, or abandoned items deliberately sunk for habitat restoration. Artificial reefs provide surfaces for corals, oysters, and barnacles to attach to, which in turn provide homes and food for other organisms.

Sunken Ships

The most commonly found artificial reefs are sunken ships. While many are submerged shipwrecks, there are also retired ships intentionally sunk and abandoned for the purpose of reef recovery. Ships prepared for an artificial reef need to be cleaned out so that no chemicals or substances are left behind that could contaminate surrounding waters.

Subway Cars

Off the coast of Delaware is Redbird Reef, named for the 600 subway cars found there. Formerly used by the New York City Redbird subway, these subway cars had their doors and windows removed before they were dumped into the ocean. Now they offer habitats and hiding spaces for numerous invertebrates, crustaceans, and fish.

Reef Balls

Reef balls are the latest kind of artificial reef, designed to withstand years in the ocean. They have been engineered with rough surfaces for corals to adhere to, and holes designed for protective spaces and continual water flow, bringing nutrients to animals and plants living on the reef ball surfaces.

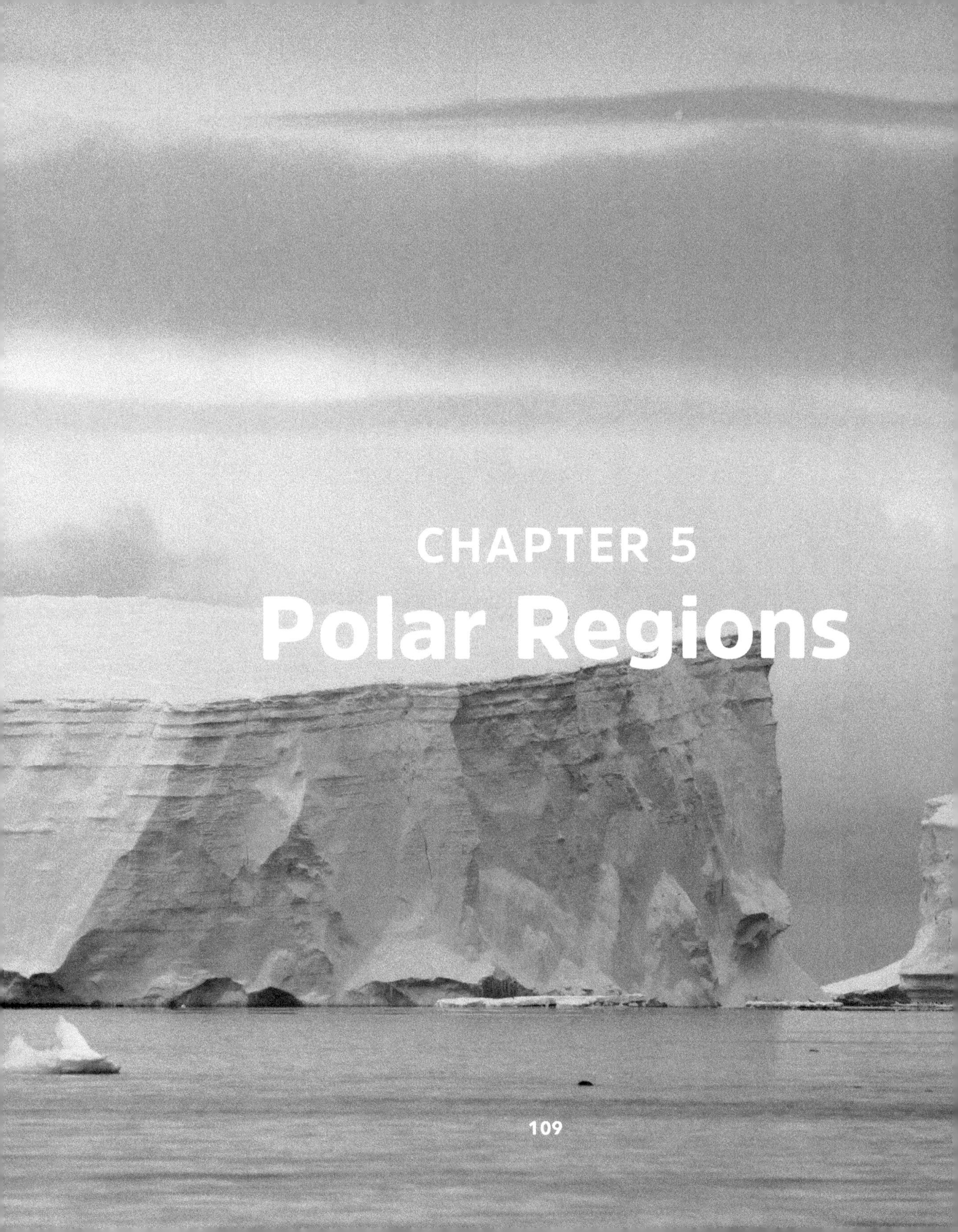

CHAPTER 5
Polar Regions

The Arctic polar region is one of the most remote places on the planet. It is home to an abundance of marine wildlife, including polar bears and walruses, which are found nowhere else on Earth. Their physical adaptations allow them to live in this harsh environment, but that is not enough. These **resident** animals, along with those that migrate through each year, rely on a healthy ocean and sea ice to sustain them.

Plankton

Plankton are the base of the Arctic food chain. They are generally very tiny plants and animals that float along using ocean currents and tides. There are two types of plankton—phytoplankton, which use sunlight for photosynthesis and produce over half of the world's oxygen, and zooplankton, which are drifting animals.

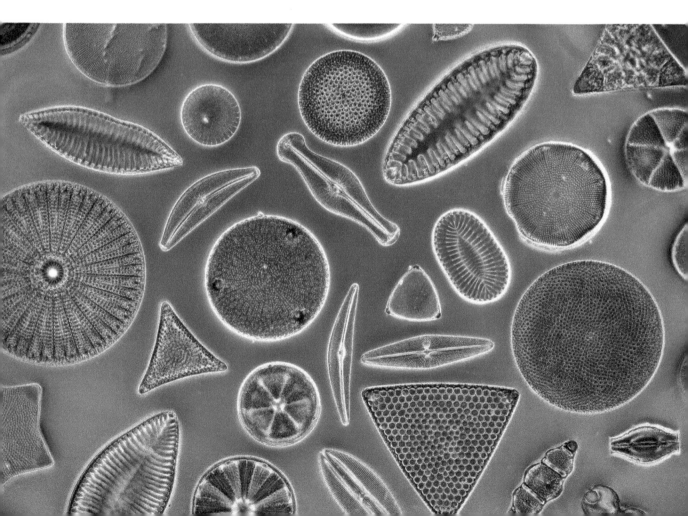

Polar Cod

One of the most abundant fish in the Arctic is the polar cod. It is an essential food source for many large mammals of the region, such as the narwhal and ringed seal. Juvenile polar cod use pack ice as a safe haven from predators and will aggressively feed on zooplankton living under the ice, growing large in a short period of time.

Arctic Char

The Arctic char is a key species in Arctic ecosystems and is related to the salmon. It is **anadromous**, meaning it migrates from the ocean to freshwater rivers to spawn. Spawning males display bellies of white, red, pink, or orange, depending on their habitat or population, or the time of year.

In the summer, 50 percent of the Arctic Ocean is covered in permanent pack ice, with an average thickness of about 10 feet (3 meters). This pack ice increases to 85 percent in the winter, and while some extends from the shore, most pack ice drifts with the current. Arctic animals have learned to use the growing and receding sea ice as their hunting grounds.

Polar Bear

Size/Weight	up to 10 ft (3 m) / 330 to 1,200 lbs (50 to 544 kg)
Diet	seals, fishes, seabirds, and eggs
Speed	25 mph (40 kph)
Status	vulnerable
Life Span	20 to 30 years

Polar Bear

Often seen roaming the winter pack ice hunting for seals, the polar bear has thick body fat and water-repellent fur that insulates it from the cold water and air. The polar bear is an excellent swimmer. It uses its paddle-like front paws to propel itself through the water while holding its hind legs flat like a boat rudder. It uses its huge paws and weight to break through snow and ice to grab seals before they can escape.

Did You Know?

The fur of a polar bear isn't white. It is transparent—see-through—with a hollow core that reflects light!

The Cubs

Polar bear cubs only weigh about 1 pound (0.5 kilograms) when they are born, so the mother polar bear gives birth in snow dens to keep the cubs protected from the harsh Arctic climate. When the cubs are about four or five months old, the family will emerge, and the mother bear will teach her cubs how to survive and hunt for food for the next two years.

Narwhal—The Unicorn of the Sea

The narwhal is a toothed whale with only two teeth. In males, one tooth grows into a sword-like spiral tusk up to 8.8 feet (2.7 meters) long. During the summer, narwhals will swim in pods of as small as 20 to up to numbers in the thousands along the ice floe edge. They use their tusks to hit, stun, and feed on fish, shrimp, and squid.

Climate Change and Arctic Animals

What We Can Do About It

Sea ice is critical to Arctic marine life. It provides an area for them to hunt, live, breed, and raise their young. Unfortunately, due to climate change, the average temperature of the Arctic has increased drastically since the 1970s, causing the sea ice to shrink. With temperatures warming, the Arctic sea ice is also freezing later in winter and breaking up earlier in the spring, leaving the sea unfrozen for longer periods of time, causing major problems for Arctic species. Here are some ways you can help minimize global warming:

1. Save energy by turning off lights, taking shorter showers, and closing doors so heat doesn't escape.

2. Suggest some ideas to your family to save energy around the house. Ideas include replacing incandescent bulbs with fluorescent ones and reducing the temperature in the house when everyone is gone for the day.

3. Start a conservation club at school. Ask teachers to help you and your friends find ways for the school to reduce energy use.

Arctic Seabirds

The number of seabirds in the Arctic fluctuates depending on the season. Most species migrate south once ice covers the water for the winter. However, in summer, breeding seabirds take advantage of the long daylight hours and hot spots of fish and zooplankton forced to the surface by **upwellings**, the process in which colder water rich in nutrients rises from the ocean depths.

Puffin

Puffins, like penguins, are excellent swimmers. Unlike penguins, they can fly. When hunting fish, puffins use their small wings to help them maneuver and chase prey underwater, sometimes diving as deep as 200 feet (60 meters). Puffins are strong fliers, but they cannot take off without a running start. Their tiny wings also make it impossible for puffins to glide while flying, so they usually rest on the surface of the ocean.

Little Auk

Just like other seabirds, the little auk needs land for mating and nesting but depends entirely on the ocean for its food. A skillful diver, the little auk will reach depths of up to 115 feet (35 meters), then shoot back to the surface in a zigzag pattern, capturing prey.

Black Guillemot

Unlike other seabirds that venture out to sea for a meal, the black guillemot prefers shallow waters near the shore. Baby guillemots, at only three weeks old, will take death-defying plunges from steep cliffs to join their fathers in the water below. There the father can feed the chicks faster.

Arctic Pinnipeds

With their barrel-shaped bodies, a thick layer of blubber to insulate them, and plenty of fish to feed on, the pinnipeds of the Arctic are well-suited to this cold and harsh environment. Many Arctic seals live in the same regions as foxes, wolves, polar bears, and humans, so they are threatened by more predators than their Antarctic relatives.

Walrus

The walrus is the largest pinniped of the Arctic Ocean. It uses its distinctive ivory tusks to ward off predators, establish dominance, and haul out on the sea ice to rest. The walrus uses its mouth like a vacuum to feed off the bottom of the ocean, sucking up shellfish, worms, crabs, and invertebrates.

Walrus

Size/Weight	7.25 to 11.5 ft (m) / up to 3,000 lbs (1,360 kg)
Diet	shellfish, crustaceans, and sea cucumbers
Speed	4.3 mph (7 kph)
Status	vulnerable
Life Span	up to 40 years

Ringed Seal

The smallest and most common Arctic seal, the ringed seal gets its name from the light-colored rings that appear on its dark fur. Ringed seals are the primary prey of polar bears, so they will use snow caves to protect and nurse their pups. When hunting, they can stay underwater for up to 45 minutes and will blow bubbles before resurfacing to check for polar bears, which will break through the ice at a sign of a seal returning.

Hooded Seal

The hooded seal has silver-gray fur and a stretchy cavity, or hood, in its nose. Adult males can inflate this hood so it looks like a bright red balloon to attract females. They also have a black bladder on their head that they can inflate to attract females or show aggression toward other males.

Although they live in water, seals must surface regularly to breathe. When the ocean is covered by several feet of ice, seals find a hole in the ice and keep it open by surfacing regularly to breathe into it, preventing it from freezing over. Here, a pup waits for its mother to return to the breathing hole.

Antarctic Polar Region

One of the most important features of the Antarctic Ocean is its Circumpolar Current. This current flows clockwise and is the only current that flows completely around the globe, keeping warm ocean waters away from Antarctica and enabling it to maintain its huge ice sheet. The Antarctic Circumpolar Current pulls cold, nutrient-rich waters from the deep sea to the surface, nourishing blooms of phytoplankton and ice algae. These feed Antarctic krill, the main food staple of larger animals like whales, penguins, and seals.

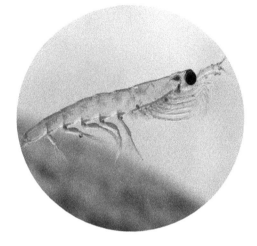

Phytoplankton

As the sunlight increases, phytoplankton "blooms" occur in the surface water of the Antarctic each year. For a few months around December, the long hours of sunlight provide perfect conditions for phytoplankton to multiply. These blooms can occur in open water or even under ice layers. They feed krill and fish, which are the primary food source for many filter feeders and penguins.

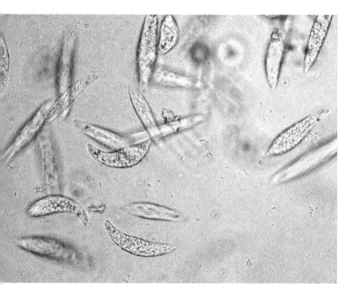

Did You Know?

The Southern Ocean giant sea spider has up to 12 legs that hold the sea spider's organs!

Krill

Krill are shrimp-like animals that, while only 2 inches (5 centimeters) in size, make a giant impact on the food webs of the Antarctic. With numbers sometimes reaching the billions, krill are the main source of energy for several animals, including fish, penguins, and blue whales. At certain times of the year, the krill get so dense that their swarms can be seen from space.

Orca: Top Predator

Commonly referred to as killer whales, orcas are found in every ocean but are most abundant in the Southern Ocean. The orca is one of the most recognizable whales with its massive black body, white underbelly, and white patch behind the eyes. Each orca also has a gray patch, called a saddle, behind its dorsal fin that is unique to each individual like a human fingerprint.

Wolves of the Sea

Orcas are called the "wolves of the sea" because they are fierce, organized hunters that travel in pods of 5 to 60 whales. Each pod communicates using unique sounds, and just like humans, they have different accents and languages. Some pods are **transient**, meaning they migrate throughout the oceans. Other pods are resident, staying in one specific habitat.

What's for Dinner?
Anything Orcas Want

Orcas have no known predators and are at the top of the marine food chain. Resident orcas mostly feed on readily available fish species such as salmon or herring. Transient orcas tend to eat a wider variety of marine animals such as squids, seals, penguins, blue whales, and even sharks. On rare occasions, they have even been known to eat moose!

Orca

Size/Weight	up to 32 ft (9.7 m) / up to 12,000 lbs (5,400 kg)
Diet	fishes, seals, sharks, whales, and squids
Speed	34 mph (56 kph)
Status	some species listed as endangered
Life Span	30 to 90 years

Penguins

The most common bird in Antarctica is the iconic penguin with its striking black and white coloring. Of the 17 species of penguin, 5 live on Antarctica—emperor, gentoo, Adélie, macaroni, and chinstrap. They live in colonies known as rookeries. It is estimated that the total number of breeding pairs on Antarctica has reached 20 million.

Penguins, which cannot fly, have evolved into the most efficient divers and swimmers of any bird. Using their short flippers to propel them underwater, and cruising at about 6 miles per hour (10 kilometers per hour), they fly through the ocean waters.

Emperor Penguin

The emperor penguin is the largest of the penguin species, some topping the scales at 100 pounds. The male emperor is the only animal to remain on the continent of Antarctica year-round. With the wind chill, temperatures can drop to −76°F (−60°C). The males huddle together, keeping their eggs warm until the females return after two months with food for the newly hatched chicks.

Emperor Penguin

Size/Weight	48 in (122 cm) / 44 to 100 lbs (20 to 45 kg)
Diet	fishes, crustaceans, and squid
Speed	1.5 mph (2.5 kph)
Status	near threatened
Life Span	15 to 20 years

Adélie Penguin

During the spring, the Adélie penguin can be found living on the coastal sea ice in colonies numbering in the thousands. There they build nests, and the parents take turns incubating the eggs, which hatch in December. At seven to nine weeks old, Adélie penguins leave the colony to go to sea and won't return until they are three to five years old.

Antarctic Seals

Seals of the Antarctic are extremely well-adapted to the region's freezing conditions, with their thick layer of blubber and dense fur. Seals are carnivorous, meaning they eat meat. Depending on the species, they will eat krill, fish, or squid. They use their whiskers, called vibrissae, to detect motion in the water. Spending most of their lives in the water, seals only come ashore to breed and raise their pups.

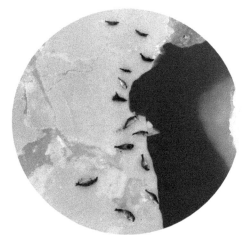

Leopard Seal

The leopard seal is a fierce hunter and one of the top predators of the Southern Ocean. It will wait underwater at the edge of the ice for penguins and other seals to enter the ocean. The most vulnerable are the young chicks and seal pups that are entering the water for the first time.

Leopard Seal

Size/Weight	8 to 11.5 ft (2.5 to 3.5 m) / 440 to 1,320 lbs (200 to 600 kg)
Diet	penguins, other seal species, krill, squid, and fishes
Speed	22 mph (37 kph)
Status	least concern
Life Span	25 years

Crabeater Seal

Despite its name, the crabeater seal does not eat crabs. It feasts mostly on krill. The crabeater seal swims through schools of krill with its mouth open, then uses its uniquely shaped teeth to filter out the water, much like a baleen whale.

Antarctic Fish

A ntarctic fish inhabit the Southern Ocean. They are remarkable in that they have adapted to live in temperatures close to the freezing point of seawater. Many are able to survive with the help of a chemical in their blood that doesn't allow their blood to freeze. Antarctic fish are considered **stenotherms**, or organisms that can only survive in a narrow range of temperatures. For this reason, Antarctic fish are particularly vulnerable to climate change.

Icefish

Icefish inhabit the coldest waters of the world's oceans. They are the only vertebrate—an animal with a backbone—that lacks hemoglobin, the protein that gives blood its red color. Because of this, icefish appear to have white blood.

Antarctic Toothfish

Toothfish are large bottom dwellers found at depths ranging from 980 to 9,800 feet (300 to 3,000 meters). Growing to lengths of over 7.5 feet (2.3 meters), these fish prey on smaller fish but are known to eat squid and crustaceans as well. Recent research just revealed that these fish can live to be 50 years old.

Snailfish

The snailfish, also called the sea snail, is a tadpole-shaped fish that has a soft, gelatinous body with no scales. Scientists have marveled at how a fish that seems so fragile-looking can exist at extreme depths of 23,000 to 27,000 feet (7,000 to 8,200 meters) and thrive there.

Eelpout

The eelpout has a long, slender body and thick lips, resembling an eel. It is also very slimy. Under its chin is a long, fleshy feeler called a **barbel**, which looks a lot like a goatee. Eelpouts are **benthic**, meaning they live on the bottom and use their barbels to detect vibrations and catch their prey.

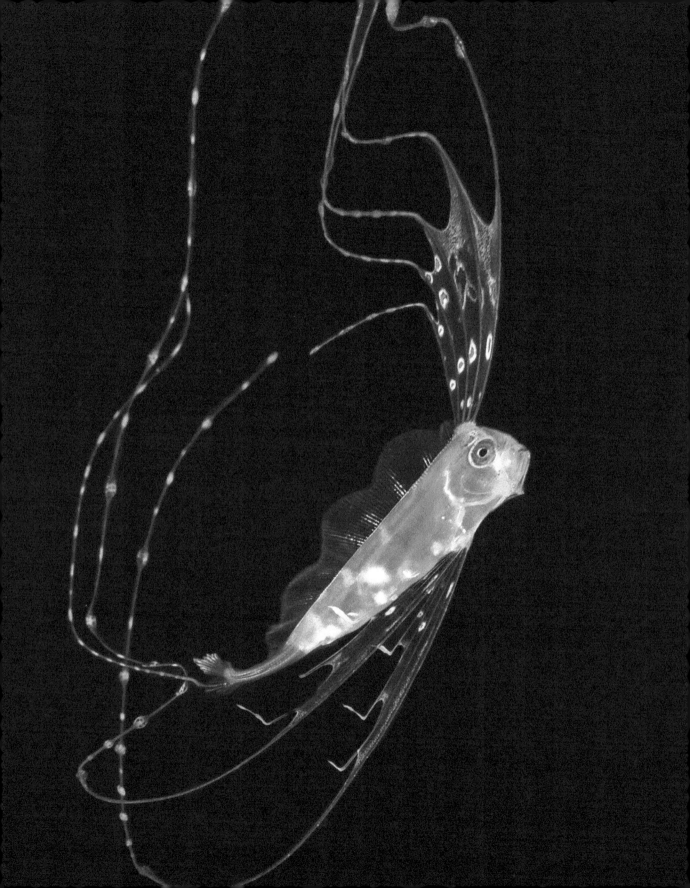

CHAPTER 6

Deep Waters and the Ocean Floor

Deep Waters and the Ocean Floor

The deep sea is a mysterious world that is still largely unexplored. Taking up 95 percent of Earth's living space, the water below the ocean's surface has already intrigued many with its bizarre creatures and harsh environment. Dive deep and not only does the light fade to complete darkness, but the drop in temperature and increase in pressure would kill most creatures on this planet. However, thousands of fascinating animals have adapted to survive in this complex environment.

Twilight Zone

Sunlight is scattered as it shines toward the ocean depths. At about 660 feet (200 meters) below the surface, a hint of blue light is all that can reach, marking the top of the twilight zone, which extends to about 3,300 feet (1,000 meters). In this zone, most animals rely on the sunlight zone above for food. They either wait until nightfall to swim up and hunt or wait for scraps to float down from above. Some animals will stay put and ambush their unlucky prey.

Glass Squid

The 60 species of glass squid are named this for their completely **transparent** or see-through skin, which helps keep them hidden from predators. Most glass squids have incredibly short arms, and the only visible parts of their bodies are their eyes. They are able to hide these as well, using two photophores under their eyes to give off a glow. This trick is called **counterillumination**.

Hatchetfish

The hatchetfish, named for its hatchet-like body shape, is covered in tiny silvery scales. When waiting for food to fall from above, the hatchetfish uses its large, tube-shaped eyes that always point upward to distinguish shadows from the faint light of the surface.

Lanternfish

The lanternfish is one of many deepwater fish that have organs called photophores, which give off light. The photophores are located on the fish's head, underbelly, and tail, which it uses to attract smaller fish to feed on and to find a mate.

Blobfish

The blobfish is a very goopy fish with a gloomy-looking face. This harmless fish doesn't have bones, teeth, or a swim bladder, which allows most fish to control their buoyancy in the water. Making sure to not expend energy, the blobfish will bob along the seabed, sucking up unsuspecting crabs and shellfish that cross its path.

Blobfish

Size/Weight	up to 12 in (30 cm) / 20 lbs (9 kg)
Diet	sea urchins, crustaceans, and tiny mollusks
Speed	unknown
Status	not evaluated
Life Span	unknown

Midnight Zone

The midnight zone includes some of the most bizarre creatures on the planet. With absolutely no light, crushing pressure, frigid temperatures, and thousands of feet between this zone and the base of the food chain (plankton), the midnight zone makes it a challenge for animals to find food while conserving energy. To do this, they have evolved some unique adaptations.

Deep-Sea Anglerfish

The female deep-sea anglerfish uses a lure to attract mates and prey. The lure is filled with light-producing bacteria that the anglerfish can pulse or move back and forth. When it successfully attracts small fish and crustaceans, it uses its very large mouth and sharp teeth to capture and swallow its meal.

Deep-Sea Anglerfish

Size/Weight	8 to 40 in (up to 1 m) / up to 110 lbs (50 kg)
Diet	crustaceans, shrimp, fishes, and snails
Speed	unknown
Status	not listed
Life Span	20 to 30 years

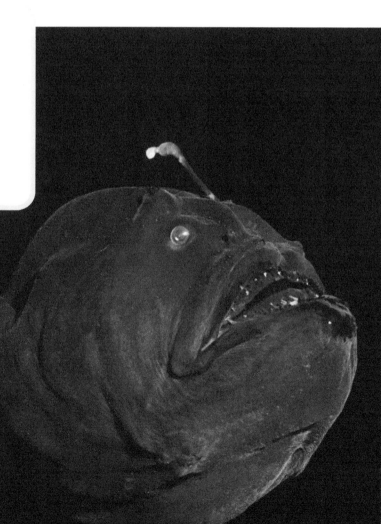

Vampire Squid

Even though the vampire squid looks familiar, it isn't an octopus or a squid. However, it *is* a close relative. The vampire squid is named for the dark skin that connects its arms, resembling a cape. When threatened, the vampire squid will turn its cape upside down, displaying large spines on the underside. Although harmless, this act makes the vampire squid look terrifying to predators.

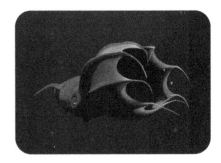

Gulper Eel

The gulper eel looks very different from most eel species. Its most notable feature is its enormous mouth, which is much larger than its body. The mouth has a pouch-like lower jaw, much like a pelican, which can hold an entire fish. The gulper eel also has a whip-like tail tipped with a photophore that glows pink to attract prey.

Barreleye Fish

No one knew that the barreleye fish really had a transparent head until researchers at the Monterey Bay Aquarium Research Institute used an underwater robot to film it almost 2,460 feet (750 m) below the ocean surface. The eyes of this fish have a special way to use what little sunlight penetrates to their depth. The eyes are split—the top half points to the ocean above, and the lower half point into the deep below. Another unusual part is that instead of a lens like most fish, the barreleye has a mirror made of stacks of crystals which help to focus the light.

Bioluminescence

In a world of darkness, organisms that live in the deep ocean have evolved the ability to use chemicals within their bodies to produce light. This process is called **bioluminescence**. While a few species on land can produce light, the deep ocean has hundreds of species equipped with light organs called photophores. The animals use the flashing of their lights for a variety of reasons such as warning other creatures to stay away, communicating, finding a mate, or even luring in prey.

Counterillumination

Most animals of the twilight zone use counterillumination, an adaptation that is very similar to countershading. To help blend into a place with very few hiding places, creatures use light from bioluminescent photophores to blend in with the sunlight filtering down from the surface.

Did You Know?

When threatened, some bioluminescent animals will break off parts of their bodies to distract predators while they crawl away in the dark.

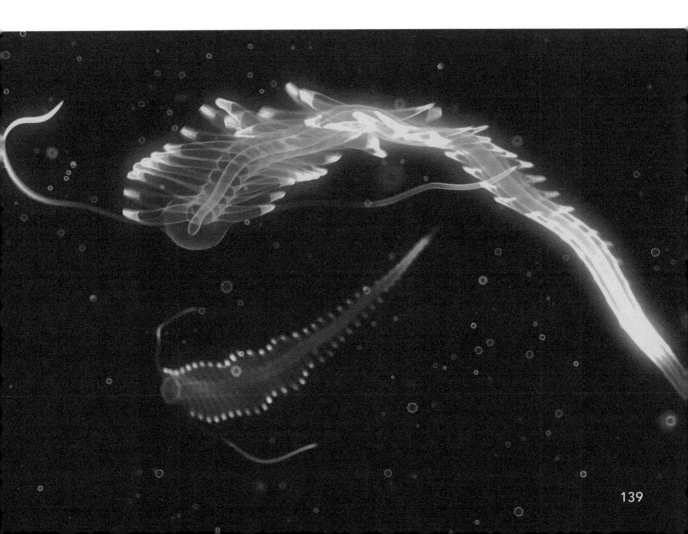

Deep-Sea Adaptations

By now, you know that marine life in the deep ocean must deal with darkness, intense pressures, and freezing temperatures. These factors are extreme, but let's not forget about the competition for food and mates, along with potential predators. These living conditions have led to fascinating adaptations that allow organisms to succeed in this ecosystem.

Body Color

Many animals use camouflage to change their skin color, matching their surroundings to stay hidden from predators. Deep-sea animals do this too, but they tend to be transparent, colorless, or black or red. Where transparent and black fish blend into the darkness, the same goes for the red animals, because red light cannot reach these depths.

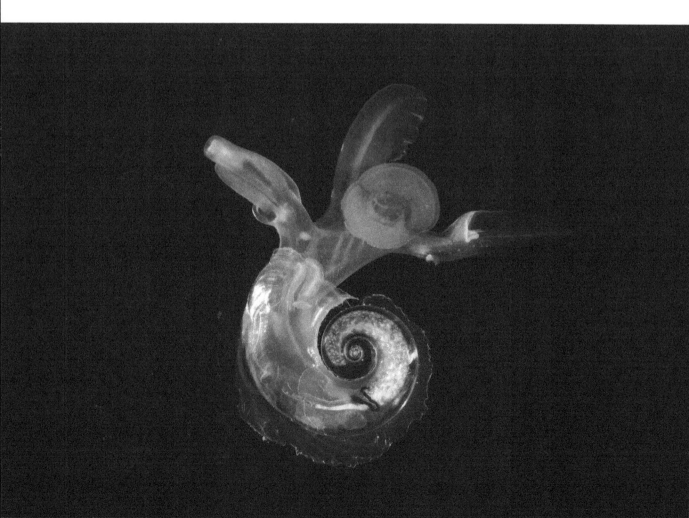

Gigantism

One adaptation that is still being studied is known as deep-sea gigantism. This phenomenon allows some animals to grow truly enormous compared to their land-dwelling relatives. Scientists believe this adaptation helps animals cover more area when searching for food and provides more energy storage between meals.

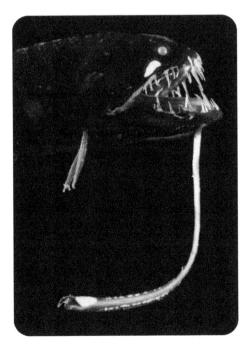

Feeding

Many deep-sea creatures have evolved feeding structures that give them a higher success rate of catching and devouring their prey. Many deep-sea fish have enormous mouths with fang-like teeth for snagging prey. Their victim is often large, so these fish also have wide-hinged jaws and expandable stomachs to hold their huge meal.

When threatened, the atolla jellyfish, also known as the alarm jelly, displays a series of bioluminescent blue flashes that circle around like lights on top of a police car. This flashy show actually draws the attention of other creatures, which will attack the potential predator as the jellyfish swims to safety.

Abyssal Zone

Conditions of the Abyssal Zone, or the Abyss, remain constant even if the seas are rough at the surface. The water is very still, and the temperature is about 39.2°F (4°C). While most of the animals here are scavengers that feed on seafloor mud and floating matter, some carnivores use unique adaptations for hunting and catching prey.

Viperfish

Despite its small size, the ferocious-looking viperfish has such enormous fangs that they don't even fit inside its mouth. These sharp teeth are used to impale the viperfish's prey, which it lures using the light-producing photophore at the tip of its long **dorsal spine**.

Tripod Fish

The tripod fish has unique fins that are longer at the tips. These are called rays. The rays stiffen when hunting and become flexible when swimming. The tripod fish will perch on the rays of its pelvic fins and wait for prey to approach. The rays of its pectoral fins act as hands, reaching out to capture food and directing it toward the tripod fish's mouth.

Giant Squid

The largest giant squid on record was almost 43 feet (13 meters) in length, definitely earning its name. Like all squids, the giant squid has eight arms and two tentacles, which it uses to catch prey. After catching prey, the arms guide the food toward its powerful, sharp beak, which slices it into pieces.

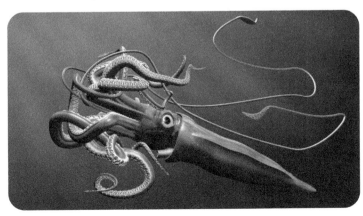

Did You Know?

The giant squid has two feeding tentacles armed with hundreds of powerful, sharp-toothed suckers, which it can shoot out up to 33 feet (10 meters) to snatch prey!

Mariana Trench

Scientific expeditions have been surprised at the diverse life surviving in the depth and harsh conditions of the Mariana Trench. More than 7 miles (11.2 kilometers) deep and five times the length of the Grand Canyon, this crescent-shaped trench boasts the deepest point in the ocean—Challenger Deep. Food is very limited in the Mariana Trench; there are lots of scavenging species, which serve as the main food source for those higher on the food chain.

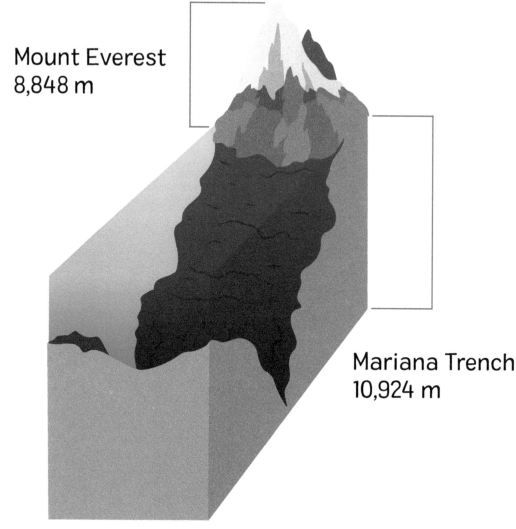

Mount Everest
8,848 m

Mariana Trench
10,924 m

Supergiant Amphipod

Amphipods are shrimp-like crustaceans that are usually less than a half an inch (1 centimeter) in size, but supergiant amphipods found in the deep sea can reach 13 inches (34 centimeters) in length—that's 20 times larger!

Ping-Pong Tree Sponge

The ping-pong tree sponge is one of several carnivorous sponges that have been discovered or photographed by the Monterey Bay Aquarium Research Institute using high-tech underwater robots. Standing about 20 inches (50 cm) high, it has large globes that radiate from its body. The globes are covered with sticky material and hooks, like Velcro, to catch prey such as small crustaceans. Eventually, the prey is engulfed and slowly digested.

Zombie Worm

When dead whales sink to the bottom of the ocean, the zombie worm consumes the part that most creatures can't—the bones. The zombie worm secretes an acid that helps it get to the center of the bones, then uses symbiotic bacteria to convert the bone's marrow into nutrients to eat.

Dumbo Octopus

There are 15 species of dumbo octopus, which belong to a group of umbrella octopus. These particular umbrella octopuses have fins that resemble elephants' ears, hence the name. Dumbo octopuses flap these fins to slowly move along the seafloor, using their arms to steer.

Seamounts

Seamounts are extinct volcanoes that rise thousands of feet from the seafloor. They are commonly found along tectonic plates. Seamounts help us learn about the geological forces that have shaped the Earth. Their massive size creates obstacles that affect ocean currents and direct deep, nutrient-rich waters up their steep slopes, making seamounts attractive habitats for marine life.

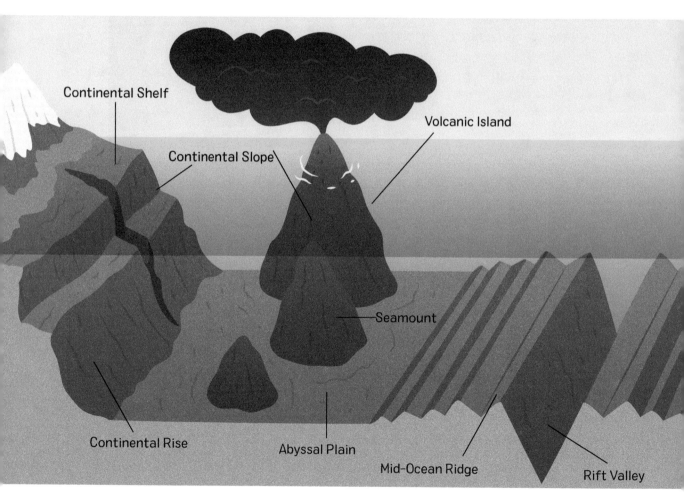

Continental Shelf

Continental Slope

Volcanic Island

Seamount

Continental Rise

Abyssal Plain

Mid-Ocean Ridge

Rift Valley

Oasis of Life

Seamounts function as an "oasis of life," having a diverse number of marine animals living on them compared to the surrounding sea-floor. This is because they can provide a much better location for attachment for organisms to settle and grow. These organisms then provide a food source for other animals, creating a unique habitat.

Dominant Organisms of Seamounts

Water is continuously flowing fast around and over seamounts, carrying food particles for filter feeders like corals and sponges, the most dominant organisms in seamount communities. Many species have formed relationships with the sponges and corals. Dumbo octopuses attach eggs to a few coral species, and juvenile worms affect how coral grows its branches to create a tunnel for the worm to live.

Guyot

When seamounts have their tops flattened over time due to erosion, then sink back into the deep water, a **guyot** (pronounced gee-OH) is formed. Guyots' flat tops form a stable habitat for animals to live, resulting in a significant variety of species. Unfortunately, these flat tops make it easier for illegal mining and fishing, so conservation efforts are necessary.

Seamount rises above water

Erosion by waves flattens the top of the mount

The seamount becomes submerged to form a guyot

Hydrothermal Vents

Scientists discovered **hydrothermal vents** in 1977, along with an unexpected community of animals thriving around them. These undersea hot springs are indeed very hot—anywhere from 50°F (10°C) to 660°F (350°C)! Hydrothermal vents are produced when cold water seeps down through the ocean floor toward the mantle. It is heated, then forced back up through the Earth's crust as a product of tectonic activity and underwater volcanoes.

With zero sunlight to photosynthesize, the primary producers around hydrothermal vents are bacteria that make their own food using chemicals in a process called **chemosynthesis**. These bacteria are the base of the food chain in the hydrothermal vent community.

Black Smoker

When water, rich with minerals, is forced through the vents, it mixes with the surrounding ocean water and cools rapidly. This causes many of the minerals to solidify and build up, forming a chimney-like structure around the vents called a **black smoker**. The black "smoke" released by the vents is a dense cloud of mineral particles.

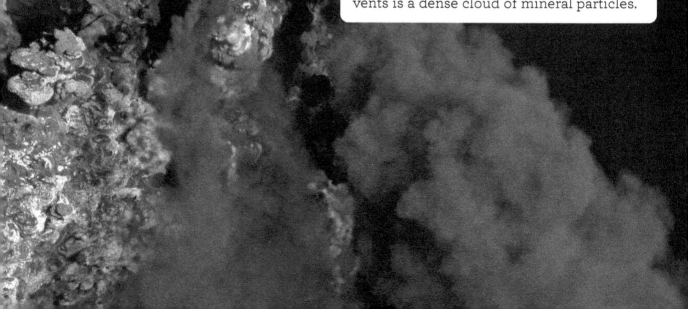

Giant Tubeworm

Reaching 6 feet (1.8 meters) long, the giant tubeworm is one of the most impressive animals living around hydrothermal vents. It uses its bright red gills to absorb vent-produced chemicals into its blood, which is delivered to bacteria colonies living inside it. The bacteria can process the chemicals into food for both themselves and the worm.

Extremophiles

Archaea are similar to bacteria and are among the simplest and most primitive forms of life. Scientists have discovered groups of archaea living in hydrothermal vents with their high temperatures and toxic chemicals seeping from them. For this reason, these archaea are considered **extremophiles** for the extreme nature of their environments.

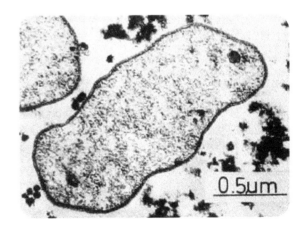

Deep-Sea Exploration

The challenges of the deep ocean—complete darkness, crushing pressures, and freezing temperatures—limit divers, sensors, and satellites from exploring its mysteries. Over the last few decades, engineers have developed technologies that can meet many of these challenges. Now marine biologists and geologists have access to ocean depths that were once impossible to explore. These advancements not only improve our understanding of this vast wilderness but also help us, as humans, understand what and how we need to protect these ecosystems and their inhabitants.

Did You Know?

As it was preparing to launch, a research submersible named *Alvin* snapped from its cable, dropping to the bottom of the sea. When it was retrieved 10 months later, the crew members' lunches were perfectly preserved thanks to the freezing temperatures.

Deep-Sea Submersibles

While there are some submersibles driven by people, most deep ocean exploration is done by two types of robots—remotely operated vehicles, or ROVs, and autonomous underwater vehicles, or AUVs. Both deep-sea submersibles are capable of collecting data such as detailed maps of the seafloor, photographs, and temperature and salinity readings. The plus side of AUVs is that they can navigate huge distances without human control. Piloted ROVs can not only send back a live video feed, but the human pilot can also manipulate robotic arms to collect samples of rocks or ocean life.

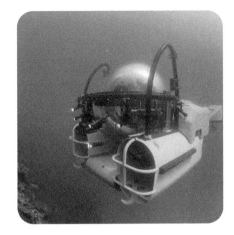

Underwater Observatories

While deep-sea submersibles are vital to deep ocean research, they still only provide a snapshot of the environment. Scientists are turning to underwater observatories that can be left in a specified location for extended periods to monitor marine life and the overall health of the environment. These observatories are covered in sensors that do everything from measuring water temperature to taking photos of sea life, and even recording calls of marine mammals.

Glossary

abdomen: part of the body with digestive organs; the belly

algin: chemical found in brown algae used in food and medicine

anadromous: migrating from saltwater to freshwater to breed

archaea: simple single-celled organism that is able to live in extreme and harsh environments

artificial reef: human-made coral reef

atoll: coral reef that develops a ring around a central lagoon

barbel: a thin piece of flesh growing from the lip or snout of a fish

barrier reef: coral reef that develops at some distance away from the coast

benthic: living on the bottom

biodiversity: variety of life on Earth

bioluminescence: production of light by living organisms

black smoker: hydrothermal vent that ejects heated water containing black chemical matter

carnivore: animal that feeds on meat

chemosynthesis: making one's own food using chemicals

cnidarian: group of invertebrates that includes jellyfish and sea anemones

commensalism: type of symbiotic relationship in which one species benefits and the other species is neither helped nor harmed

continental shelf: shallow underwater floor surrounding a continent

coral bleaching: the removal of zooxanthellae by reef corals in response to stress

counterillumination: the use of bioluminescence to blend in with light

crustacean: member of a group of marine life that includes lobsters, crabs, crayfish, shrimp, and barnacles

detritus: wastes and remains of dead organisms

dorsal fin: fin on the back of a fish or whale

dorsal spine: rigid structure that supports dorsal fins

echolocation: ability of some animals to sense their surroundings using sound waves, or clicks, they emit

ecosystem: community of living organisms and the nonliving features that support them in an environment

erosion: the action of wind, water, or other natural agents that remove soil, rock, or dissolved material from one location on the Earth's crust, and then transport it to another location

estuary: body of water where a river meets the ocean

exoskeleton: skeleton that forms the external surface of an animal

extinction: a coming to an end or dying out of a species

extremophile: microorganism that lives in extreme conditions of temperature, acidity, alkalinity, or chemical concentration

fertilize: to make an egg able to grow and develop

filter feeder: an organism that actively filters food particles

fissure: a long break in rock or earth made by cracking or splitting

food web: pattern of interacting food chains

fringing reef: coral reef that develops as a narrow band close to shore

guyot: seamount with flattened top

gyre: large, nearly circular system of wind-driven surface currents that center on latitude 30° in both hemispheres

herbivore: animal that eats plants

hydrothermal vent: opening in the seafloor out of which heated, mineral-rich water flows

intertidal zone: area between the highest and lowest tide

invasive species: a living thing that is introduced to a new environment and typically causes damage to its new ecosystem

invertebrate: animal that lacks a backbone

isopod: small, flattened crustacean

jet stream: long, powerful current of wind

keystone species: species on which other species in an ecosystem depend, such that if it were removed, the ecosystem would change drastically

latitude: measurement of distance north or south of the Equator and is measured by imaginary lines that form circles around the Earth east to west

longitude: measurement east or west of the prime meridian and is measured by imaginary lines that run around the Earth vertically (up and down) and meet at the North and South Poles

monsoon: winds in the northern Indian Ocean that blow from the southwest in summer and from the northwest in winter

mutualism: type of symbiotic relationship in which both partners benefit

navigate: to travel by water

nematocyst: stinging part on a tentacle of a cnidarian

niche: unique living arrangement of an organism defined by its habitat, food sources, time of day it is most active, and other factors

nocturnal: active at night

nonpoint source pollution: complex combination of pollutants rather than one identifiable source

omnivorous: eating both plants and animals

organism: living thing

paralysis: loss of the ability to move (and sometimes to feel anything) in part or most of the body, typically as a result of illness, poison, or injury

parasitism: type of symbiotic relationship where one species benefits and the other is harmed

pectoral fin: each of the pair of fins just behind the head of fishes

photophore: an organ that produces bioluminescence (light)

photosynthesis: chemical process that turns sunlight into food using carbon dioxide and water

pod: a school of whales, dolphins, or porpoises

polychaete: segmented worm that typically has paired bristle-like legs

polyp: cylindrical body, typically that of a cnidarian

pores: tiny holes that lead to the inside of a sponge

pressure: the amount of force pushing down on something else

primary consumer: organism that feeds directly on producers

producer: organism that makes its own food

radial symmetry: having similar parts arranged around a central point

remora: a small, slender fish that attaches itself to larger animals using suction

resident: living in one place for an extend amount of time

rostrum: a long projecting nose

runoff: draining away of water from the surface of an area of land

salinity: total amount of salt dissolved in seawater

scavenger: animal that feeds on detritus

sclerite: hard plate or spine

seamount: underwater mountain, usually a dormant volcano

secondary consumer: animal that eats primary consumers

sediment: matter that settles to the bottom of a liquid

semilunar tide: highest tides occuring twice a month, at the times of the new and full moons every two weeks

siphon: to draw or move water using a tube-like extension of bivalves and cephalopods, and in tunicates

siphonophore: a colony of free-swimming or floating cnidarians that are mostly delicate, transparent, and colored and have individual organisms possessing specialized functions such as feeding or locomotion

spawning: releasing eggs into the water

stenotherm: organism that can only survive in a narrow range of temperatures

surface temperature: temperature of the water at the surface of the ocean

symbiotic relationship: a close relationship between two species

tectonic plates: giant slabs of rock, or plates, that make up the layer of the Earth and move a few centimeters each year

terrestrial: relating to the land

tertiary consumer: animal that eats secondary consumers

transient: staying for only a short time

transparent: see-through

trophic level: each step in a food chain

tsunami: a long, fast wave produced by earthquakes and other seismic disturbances

tunic: a membrane covering sea squirts

tunicate: marine invertebrate surrounded by a tunic

upwelling: movement of deeper water toward the surface

venom: poisonous substance secreted by animals

venomous: able to produce a toxic substance and inject it into other animals by biting or stinging

zooxanthellae: tiny organisms that live within the tissues of reef corals and other marine animals

Resources

Books About the Ocean and Ocean Conservancy

The Big Book of the Blue by Yuval Zommer

Marine Science for Kids: Exploring and Protecting Our Watery World by Bethanie Hestermann and Josh Hestermann

National Audubon Society Guide to Marine Mammals of the World by Randall R. Reeves

National Audubon Society Field Guide to North American Seashore Creatures by Norman A. Meinkoth

Save the Ocean by Bethany Stahl

Websites and Organizations for Kids

AllAboutBirds.org
All About Birds is a free resource created by the Cornell Lab of Ornithology where you'll find detailed information on more than 600 North American bird species, including seabirds. You can also use the site for live cams to watch birds, nests, and more!

ClimateKids.nasa.gov
An interactive website that teaches younger kids about weather and climate, the ocean, the carbon cycle, and energy usage. Students are able to engage through educational crafts, games, and instructional videos, and learn how to teach others about what they have learned.

Kids.NationalGeographic.com/explore/nature/kids-vs-plastic
Plastic water bottles, straws, and bags might be part of your everyday life. But that single-use plastic doesn't disappear when you're done with it. Most ends up in the ocean, where it can entangle animals or make them sick. But you can help solve this problem. Take the Kids vs. Plastic pledge to get your Planet Protector certificate and find out what you can do to fight trash.

MontereyBayAquarium.org/animals-and-exhibits
Discover incredible animals from land and sea in this special exhibition featuring creatures from the coastal habitats of Baja California. Life here thrives on the edge of sand and surf, where rugged desert coastline meets the sapphire waters of the Pacific.

OceanToday.noaa.gov
Ocean Today is an exciting multimedia kiosk that features videos on all aspects of the ocean realm, exploration and discoveries, marine life, and science.

Sanctuaries.noaa.gov/education/ocean_guardian/resources.html
This page lists a variety of resources with all kinds of information to help enrich, inspire, and support your Ocean Guardian School Project.

Index

Photo Credits

Alamy Stock Photo: p. 6 bottom: Daniel J. Rao; p. 8 bottom: Peter Hermes Furian; p. 10 bottom: Hemis; p. 11: David South; p. 21 bottom: Nature Picture Library; p. 22 bottom: Nature Picture Library; p. 23 bottom: BIOSPHOTO; p. 25 top: Kelvin Aitken / VWPics; p. 26 top: blickwinkel; pp. 25-26: middle: Paulo Oliveira; p. 27 bottom: WaterFrame; p. 30 top: Rolf Hicker Photography; p. 31 top: Robert Bannister; p. 33 top: WorldFoto; p. 33 bottom: Stephen Frink Collection; p. 34 bottom left: Don Mammoser; p. 34 top right: Philip Mugridge ; p. 36 top: Image Source; p. 36 bottom: Carlos Villoch - MagicSea.com; p. 37 bottom: Paulo Oliveira; p. 38 bottom: imageBROKER; p. 39 WaterFrame; p. 40: Reinhard Dirscherl; p. 41: Wildestanimal, p. 41 bottom: Michael Greenfelder; p. 42 bottom: blickwinkel; p. 46 top: robertharding; p. 46 bottom: Universal Images Group North America LLC; p. 47 middle: robertharding; p. 48 top: Don Johnston_BI; p. 49 top: Brian Kushner; p. 50 top: Nature Picture Library; p. 50 bottom: Frans Lanting Studio; p. 51: Waterframe; pp. 54-55: Brandon Cole Marine Photography; p. 56 top: Blue Planet Archive; p. 56 bottom: Stocktrek Images, Inc.; p. 57 top: Mark Conlin; p. 57 bottom: Ashley Missen; p. 58 top right: Nature Picture Library; p. 59 top: Peter Llewellyn; p. 59 bottom: David Fleetham; p. 60 top: Waterframe; p. 60 bottom: Carver Mostardi; p. 61 bottom: Joe Belanger; p. 62 top right: Jeff Rotman; p. 62 bottom left: National Geographic Image Collection; p. 63 top: Mark Conlin / VWPics; p. 63 bottom: Barbara Ash; pp. 64-65: Loop Images Ltd; p. 69 top: Arterra Picture Library; p. 70 bottom: Mark Conlin; p. 71 bottom: Paulo Oliveira; p. 72 top right: Jonathan Nnguyen; p. 72 bottom left: robertharding; p. 74 bottom: Stocktrek Images, Inc.; p. 75 top: Crystite; pp. 76-77: RGB Ventures/ SuperStock; p. 78 top: Dominique Braud/Dembinsky Photo Associates; p. 79 top: Jeff Rotman; p. 79 bottom: Jason Bazzano; p. 80: Mauritius Images GmbH; p. 81 top: WaterFrame; p. 81 middle: Dominique Braud/Dembinsky Photo Associates; p. 81 bottom: All Canada Photos; p. 82: Waterframe; p. 83: Reinhard Dirscherl; p. 84: Stephen Frink Collection; p. 85 top: Michael Patrick O'Neill; p. 91 bottom: Magnus Larsson; p. 92: Waterframe; p. 93: Images & Stories; p. 94: robertharding; p. 95 top: Credit: Reinhard Dirscherl; p. 96 top: Gerald Robert Fischer; p. 97 bottom: imageBROKER; pp. 98-99: Stephen Frink Collection; p. 101 bottom: Ellen McKnight; p. 102: imageBROKER; p. 103: Chris Gug; p. 104 top: Ron Steiner; p. 105 top: ArteSub; p. 105 bottom: Helmut Corneli; p. 106; imageBROKER; p. 110: Scenics & Science ; p. 111 bottom: blickwinkel; p. 113 top: Andre Gilden; p. 115 top: Phil Crosby; p. 116 top: Andrew Woodward; p. 117 top: AGAMI Photo Agency; p. 117 bottom: WILDLIFE GmbH; pp. 118-119: Juniors Bildarchiv GmbH; p. 120 top right: Dmytro Pylypenko; p. 121: National Geographic Image Collection; p. 122: Nature Picture Library; 124 top: Roger Clark; p. 124 bottom: blickwinkel; p. 125:

Acknowledgments

We each have an excellent support team behind us, and this book wouldn't have been possible without mine.

To my husband, Dan, who knew the time demands of this book. You didn't hesitate a nanosecond before you fully supported me to take on this passion project. I now have so many more exciting ocean facts to share on our future beachcombing walks.

To my girls, Ava and Dani, who cheered me on and shared their enthusiasm of the ocean with me as we sat around the dinner table, always discussing the animals and ecosystems I was researching. To my little man, Lincoln, I can't wait for you to be able to join in these discussions. For now, just enjoy using a fork and playing with the meow-meow.

To my closest friend (who lives too far away) Erin, who always picks up the phone, has my back, and is willing to go along on any crazy adventure with me.

To all my family and friends who have supported me—it looks like we have another reason to celebrate! Get your party hats on. Cheers!

Thank you to my editor and animal enthusiast, Cathy Hennessy, for believing in me on this project. It was a tremendous opportunity to work with you and your remarkable team.

Finally, to all of the readers, thanks for sharing my passion for the ocean and all the wacky and perfect animals that live in it. I hope you had as much fun with this book as I have!

About the Author

 Dr. Erica Colón is a National Board Certified Teacher who taught science in the classroom for over a dozen years and established a marine biology program for upperclassmen at her final position. She earned her doctorate in curriculum and instruction and began to work with pre-service science teachers. Over time, Dr. Colón decided to design her own science curriculum to help teachers spend less time trying to make their own resources and focus on what they love to do most—teach. In 2012, she started her own business, Nitty Gritty Science, LLC. Her science curriculum can be found in classrooms all over the world. Dr. Colón is a proud Navy wife who lives in Virginia with her husband and three children, who all love and appreciate the ocean and its inhabitants.

Printed in the USA
CPSIA information can be obtained
at www.ICGtesting.com
CBHW052002010424
6165CB00003B/3